Stumped!

NICHOLAS HOBBES

STUMPED!

The Sports Fan's Book of Answers

Atlantic Books
LONDON

First published in Great Britain in 2007 by
Atlantic Books, an imprint of Grove Atlantic Ltd.

9 8 7 6 5 4 3 2 1

A CIP catalogue record for this book is available
from the British Library.

ISBN: 978 1 84354 665 8

Text design by Lindsay Nash
Diagrams © Mark Rolfe Technical Art

Cricket diagrams redrawn by permission of
Dr. Rabindra D. Mehta.

Printed in Great Britain by
Clays Ltd, St Ives plc

Atlantic Books
An imprint of Grove Atlantic Ltd
Ormond House
26–27 Boswell Street
London WC1N 3JZ

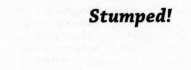

Stumped!

Contents

Acknowledgements

Special thanks are owed to Mathew Hodkin for his all-round sporting knowledge and to Charlotte Foley for her understanding of medicine and statistics.

Thanks also go to Rob Bowyer, Daniel Ghossain, Peter Harris, Carolyne Hodkin, Tom Keating , Raj Patel and Richard Wood-Wilson for their advice and to Sarah Castleton, Stuart Evers and Sarah Norman for their work in editing and improving this book.

What makes something a sport rather than a pastime?

On 24 March 2005, Sport England officially recognized darts as a sport. Some thought it ridiculous that a game played by men of doubtful health should be given such a status, but for the darts world it was long-awaited vindication of their efforts. The British Darts Organisation had employed a major law firm, consulted medical advisers and lobbied MPs as part of its campaign. The argument that finally swayed the authorities was the evidence that a darts player walks up to sixteen miles over the course of a tournament. It might seem odd that in order to change the definition of darts from a game to a sport, they lobbied the managers of Sport England rather the editorial board of the Oxford English Dictionary. Then again, unlike English sport's governing body the OED does not dish out billions of pounds of National Lottery and taxpayers' money to its favoured causes. Yet one still wonders how a press release comprising a total of 248 words from a little-known quango could have the power to transform a pub game into a fully fledged sport with pretensions to Olympic status.

Chess, bridge and holding one's breath underwater ('static apnoea') are all officially recognized as sports by the International Olympic Committee. Perhaps the fiat of such an august body is enough to render an activity a sport – rather like the way the curators of the Royal Academy can decide that any object is a 'work of art'. Unfortunately, the IOC does not give its criteria for accepting an activity as a sport, or offer any kind of definition. According to the philosopher Ludwig Wittgenstein, this is just as well, because any attempt to put one's finger on the essence of sport would be doomed to failure. In his view, activities from tennis and chess to ring-a-ring-a-roses and a child bouncing a ball against a wall by himself are all 'games' because they share family resemblances – a criss-crossing network of similarities.[1] There is no one quality that all games have in common, and the same goes for sports. Neither does there have to be one for the concept of either to make sense. As Supreme Court Justice Potter Stewart once said during an obscenity hearing, 'I cannot define filth, but I know it when I see it.' So what kind of family resemblances do we find among sports?

To call something a sport is to recognize in it a certain dignity. This is why some people scoffed at the thought that darts should be considered a sport in the days when the top players drank and smoked their way through matches. It is also why some sports need to be prefixed with the word 'blood', so that we can draw special attention to our righteous disapproval. However, nobility is a vague property and there are many sports – such as pool or beach volleyball – that do not seem particularly worthy of the word. Bullfighting is also recognized as a sport even by those who deem it grievously *ig*noble. In this case, it would seem that only snobbery prevents us from calling tiddlywinks a sport.

All sports are competitive, even if one is competing only against oneself. There is no reason why we should begrudge Robinson Crusoe a 'sports day' on his island. He could try to beat his personal best time for running the length of the beach or break his own keepie-uppie record. Sports need to have mutually recognized rules, because without rules there can be no notion of winning. To compete means to compete on the same lines. This prevents a game of cops and robbers from qualifying as sport, although it is not inconceivable that it could move out of the playground and into the stadium if it was sufficiently regimented. Snakes and Ladders will never be a sport, because sports cannot be games of pure chance. But neither do they have to be games of skill, for that would disqualify powerlifting. Sports are a subset of games rather than viceversa, and to qualify as the former some form of physical prowess must be involved. There is no requirement that the physical element be especially strenuous. For example, target shooting is all about making as little movement as possible, with highly skilled marksmen even learning to fire between heartbeats.

However, if we define sport as any competitive activity that involves physical prowess, then we would have to include brass band competitions and cook-offs in the roster of sports. Certain other artistic activities are already Olympic disciplines. Figure skating and gymnastics are judged subjectively on their aesthetic merits and have no greater affinity with basketball and javelin throwing than do ballet or calligraphy. They also meet the inspired definition of a sport offered by a caller on BBC Radio Five Live as 'anything that you cannot do in normal shoes'. What makes figure skating a sport where ballet is an art form is merely the way skating is arranged for public consumption – with heats and parallel competition among skaters. If ballerinas took turns to perform pirouettes in front a panel of judges at the Olympic

Games, then ballet would clearly have an equal claim to be a sport.

It now seems that what makes something a sport rather than a game or pastime is matter of bureaucracy. And there we might leave it but for the contribution of the philosopher Bernard Suits. According to Suits, sports are 'goal-directed activities in which inefficient means are intentionally (or rationally) chosen. For example, in racing games one voluntarily goes all around the track in an effort to arrive at the finish line instead of "sensibly" cutting straight across the infield.'[2] Playing a game is a voluntary attempt to overcome unnecessary obstacles. Sport would not be sport, then, if it was not essentially pointless.

Why do cyclists shave their legs?

In the 1979 comedy *Breaking Away*, the hero's father is horrified to discover that his son shaves his legs. Fortunately, there is an innocent, heterosexual explanation: the boy's dream is to become a professional cyclist, and he's read that shaving your legs cuts down wind resistance. In truth, depilation would aid his road speed no more than the Verdi and Puccini he listens to, or the fake Italian accent he puts on in emulation of his sporting idols. Yet it remains a common misconception that aerodynamics explains the lack of body hair in the Tour de France. According to Stanford University's swimming coach Skip Kenney, swimmers who shave their entire body gain a 2 per cent boost in speed.[3] But water is far thicker than air and creates more drag. Any gain in speed for a hairless cyclist or sprinter would be so small as to be unmeasurable.

Professional cyclists claim that there are two reasons why they shave. The first is medical. They fall off their bikes more often than one might expect, and it's easier to clean out the dirt and gravel from their wounds if their legs have been shaven. Bare skin coming into contact with asphalt at 35 mph is going to tear off, so it's better that it tears off cleanly, and pulling off bandages from healed cuts is less torturous if hairs are not pulled out at the same time. The second reason is more therapeutic: the massages they receive after every stage of a race are more comfortable if they are hairless.

However, there is a third – more compelling – explanation that cyclists are less ready to talk about. The cycling writer Matt Seaton put forward the following theory in 2002: 'The real reason cyclists shave their legs is very simple: it is because everyone else does it. No one likes to make a direct admission of the fact but, secretly for all, shaving one's legs has, above all, an aesthetic dimension: it is simply how the racing cyclist should look.'[4] As every oiled bodybuilder knows, smooth, polished skin looks better and allows everyone a perfect view of all your hard work. The aesthetics argument was given extra credence during the 2003 Tour de France, when the Austrian cyclist René Haselbacher's shorts were ripped off in a fall, revealing that his shaving regimen was far more thorough than would be necessary to keep lower leg wounds clean...

Who are the biggest cheats in world football?

Michael Owen shocked football fans twice over during England's second-round tie against Argentina at the 1998 World Cup. One occasion was his brilliant solo goal, voted runner-up in a FIFA poll for the greatest strike in the history of the tournament. The other was when he went down in the box and won a penalty. Owen appeared to have done something that no English fan could remember one of their internationals doing: he had 'taken a dive'. It was unusual not just because an England player seemed to have cheated, but because he had also got away with it. The last time someone had tried anything like this was when Des Walker had attempted to pull Dennis Bergkamp's shirt off in a match against Holland five years earlier. But all Walker's impression of a tug-of-war contestant achieved was a penalty for the opposing side.

The reason English players are so hopeless at cheating is because they get so little practice at it. Brazil have won the FIFA Fair Play Award a record four times; England ranks second with two awards. The award is handed out only to teams progressing to the second round of the tournament, and twice since its inception England have failed to qualify. This makes it two out of six attempts for England and four out of eight for Brazil. Other winners have been Spain, Belgium, France and, inexplicably given their overall record, Argentina.

Among the World Cup's regular participants, South American teams have dominated the bottom of the disciplinary league since the present system of red and yellow cards was introduced in 1970. Brazil, Argentina and Uruguay have each twice had the dubious honour of finishing a World Cup with the worst record. The roll of shame also includes France, Bulgaria, Turkey and, most recently, Portugal. The five worst-offending countries have been only occasional guests at the tournament:

		Games Played	Yellow Cards	Red Cards	Points*	Points per Game
1.	Turkey	7	19	2	23	3.29
2.	Portugal	13	34	4	42	3.23
3.	Cameroon	17	39	7	53	3.19
4.	Paraguay	15	33	2	37	2.47
5.	Australia	7	13	2	17	2.43

* Yellow = 1 point, Red = 2

Turkey achieved the worst ever number of disciplinary points per game in her only appearance in a World Cup in 2002, but this provides scant evidence of the Turks' long-term intent. The records of teams that have played twenty or more games in the finals are as follows:

		Games Played	Yellow Cards	Red Cards	Points*	Points per Game
1.	Uruguay	20	44	3	50	2.50
2.	Mexico	28	55	6	67	2.39
3.	Argentina	49	92	8	108	2.20
4.	Netherlands	34	60	6	72	2.11
5.	Bulgaria	20	36	3	42	2.10

6.	Spain	26	42	1	44	1.69
7.	France	34	47	5	57	1.68
8.	Sweden	30	43	3	49	1.63
9.	Italy	57	82	5	92	1.61
10.	Germany	64	91	4	99	1.55
11.	Poland	30	42	1	44	1.47
12.	Brazil	60	74	4	82	1.37
13.	England	35	39	3	45	1.29
14.	Belgium	30	30	2	34	1.13

* Yellow = 1 point, Red = 2

Some of these statistics contradict common prejudices. The Dutch have an unexpectedly poor record at odds with their clean image. In mitigation, a single game against an especially badly behaved Portugal side in 2006 was enough to move them from fifth to fourth place. It also appears that the supposedly 'cynical' Italians cheat less often than the upstanding Swedes.

However, these figures are only for those offences noted by match officials. The craftiest operators rarely get caught, at least not by the referee. For example, after picking up an early booking against Angola in the group stage of the 2006 World Cup, Portugal's Cristiano Ronaldo somehow avoided censure throughout a string of shameless performances against Holland, England, France and Germany. After his team lost to France despite his best amateur dramatics, he had the cheek to complain that 'Everyone who saw the match could see that the referee wasn't fair. He should have shown yellow cards but he did not because Portugal is a small country.' He continued his antics even in the 'meaningless' play-off for third place, where at one point he threw himself to the ground clutching his right shin after an opponent brushed past his left thigh. He has been forced to cut out this aspect of his game in the English Premiership, where referees have proved not to be so easily fooled, but his international comeuppance had to wait until the end of the World Cup when his behaviour cost him the tournament's FIFA Young Player Award. Holger Osieck, the head of the judging panel commented that 'we want to have decent behaviour'.

A persistently dirty team also goads the opposition into retaliating and committing fouls of their own. In Germany, Ronaldo's side finished way behind in last place out of thirty-two teams in the Fair Play league, with twenty-two yellow cards and two reds in seven games. The telling detail is that they incited their opponents to commit even more infractions as far as the authorities were concerned. Teams playing Portugal garnered twenty-one yellow cards and four reds. The figures in the above table also include unjust punishments handed out to those who responded to opponents' play-acting – which Italian and Portuguese players are more likely to perpetrate than fall victim to. This is not anti-Italian or anti-Latin sentiment, but a realistic appraisal of the countries' sporting ethos. What would be called 'dirty' in England would be described in Italy as *fare il furbo*', or 'being clever'. As Gianluca Vialli puts it: 'The Italian system teaches kids to protect themselves [from cheats]. The English system doesn't accept cheating as inevitable, but condemns it as something to be eradicated. In that sense, English football strives for Utopia, while Italian football is rooted in realism – which is one step away from cynicism.'[5]

After Francis Jeffers earned Arsenal a penalty and a point against Liverpool when he tripped over an invisible leg in

December 2002, Ron 'Chopper' Harris said, 'I wouldn't be surprised if he practised diving in training. Since the foreigners came over here everyone's at it, even the English lads.' Harris's memory must have been fading, for his own contemporary, Francis Lee, still holds the record for the most penalties scored in a season – thirteen in 1972. There may also be a degree of denial, for tough tackling players like Harris are partly responsible for the relish with which many skilful forwards will take a dive. Thierry Henry, for years an honourable player, admitted to diving in the 2006 Champions League Final in retaliation for the fouls he had suffered from Barcelona's hatchet men. Football is a contact sport, and there is no doubt that even Cristiano Ronaldo's tactics are in part a reaction to rough treatment by defenders who lack the talent to stop him fairly. Sometimes a player has to dive if by not doing so he would be fouled. For example, Steven Gerrard, who has acquired something of a reputation as a diver for his club side, won a penalty for England in a friendly against Hungary in May 2006 after going down in the box even though the defender's ferocious challenge had not made contact. Had he stayed on his feet there would still have been a penalty, but he might have had a broken leg to go with it. However, safety is not always the only concern for the English. Glenn Hoddle apparently felt no conflict with his Christian values when he reportedly advised Michael Owen not to try too hard to stay on his feet.

Three English players have been sent off during World Cup Finals, but even this record has been exacerbated by South American involvement. David Beckham was sent off against Argentina in 1998 for a kick aimed at Diego Simeone. Simeone collapsed in mock agony and later admitted feigning injury:

Let's just say the referee fell into the trap. It was also a difficult one for him to have avoided because I went down well and in moments like that there's a lot of tension. You could say that my falling transformed a yellow card into a red card. But in fact, the most appropriate punishment was a yellow one. Obviously, I was being clever. By letting myself fall, I got the referee to pull out a red card immediately. In reality, it wasn't a violent blow, it was just a little kick back with no force behind it, and was probably instinctive.[6]

Incredibly, he told the *Observer*'s correspondent: 'I took advantage of that. And I think anyone would have taken advantage of that in just the same way.'[7]

In Argentina, Diego Maradona's 'Hand of God' is celebrated without embarrassment, even though he admitted on national television that his handball was deliberate. The lack of shame is just as well, because the country has racked up more red and yellow cards than any other in the history of the World Cup. In Italia '90 alone they accumulated twenty-two yellow cards and three reds in seven games before losing in the final when they found their own tactics used against them. A dumbfounded Pedro Monzon became the first player to be sent off in a World Cup Final after Jurgen Klinsmann executed a virtuoso dive comprising an acrobatic arc and several rolls along the ground. Better, or worse, was to come in the 1998 quarter-final against Holland. Ariel Ortega was booked after being judged to have dived in the eighty-eighth minute, but he was so incensed at not receiving a penalty that he leapt to his feet and headbutted the opposing goalkeeper, Edwin van der Sar. Van der

Sar duly made his own meal of the situation with the result that Ortega was sent off.

At the least the Hand of God was complemented by the movement in which Maradona took the ball from the halfway line and dribbled past five English players to score the greatest of World Cup goals. 'Thanks to England,' said Maradona, 'I scored the best goal of my life, in a World Cup, a dream goal, a beautiful, precious goal. I don't think I could have done it against any other team because they all used to knock you down... The English are probably the noblest in the world.' At least noble enough to admit, as Terry Fenwick later did, that had he not already been on a yellow card he would probably have hacked the Argentinian down.

Can white men run?

I magine that you are a 13-year-old boy who excels at sport. You are the fastest sprinter in your class and lead the school team at track meetings. Your ambition is to one day win gold in the 100 metres at the Olympics, yet although your coach gives you every encouragement, he knows that you do not stand a chance of realizing your dreams and secretly hopes that you will transfer your interests to a different event. The problem is that you are white. The half-Jamaican writer Malcolm Gladwell knew such a boy in his youth:

> When I started running, there was a quarter-miler just a
> few years older than I was by the name of Arnold Stotz.
> He was a bulldog of a runner, hugely talented, and each
> year that he moved through the sprinting ranks he
> invariably broke the existing 400-metre record in his
> age class. Stotz was white, though, and every time I saw
> the results of a big track meet I'd keep an eye out for his
> name, because I was convinced that he could not keep
> winning. It was as if I saw his whiteness as a
> degenerative disease, which would eventually claim and
> cripple him. I never asked him whether he felt the same
> anxiety, but I can't imagine that he didn't. There was
> only so long that anyone could defy the rules. One day,

at the provincial championships, I looked up at the
results board and Stotz was gone.[8]

In recent decades, greater freedom for diverse groups to participate in sport has led to less diversity on winners' podiums. Not a single white man has run the 100 metres in under ten seconds without wind assistance, yet more than forty black men have done so. When Jon Entine wrote his definitive book on the subject, *Taboo: Why Black Athletes Dominate Sports and Why We're Afraid to Talk About It*,[9] athletes of West African descent had recorded all but six of the 500 best times in the 100 metres. At the outset it would seem that there is clear inequity in the way Nature hands out her gifts. It does not work solely against whites, for Indian, Chinese, Japanese and even East African athletes also try in vain to overcome their physiological disadvantage in sprinting. Since Alan Wells benefited from the US boycott of the 1980 Olympics to win 100 metres gold, every men's Olympic champion and world champion over the distance has hailed from West African stock. East Africans at least get their chance over longer distances, and their twin domination means that an athlete of African descent currently holds the men's world record in every distance contested at the Olympics, long and short.

In the United States, African Americans make up around 13 per cent of the population, yet they comprise nearly 90 per cent of the professional basketball players, 75 per cent of NFL rosters and around a third of Major League baseball players. The scale of black sporting achievement is extraordinary and undeniable. The possible reasons behind it are altogether more controversial. This is a subject that some people find impossible to discuss rationally. White liberals often cannot tolerate it being so much as broached. In 1995, Sir Roger Bannister, now a neurologist, told the British Association for the Advancement of Science: 'I am prepared to risk political incorrectness by drawing attention to the seemingly obvious but under-stressed fact that black sprinters and black athletes in general all seem to have certain natural anatomical advantages. Perhaps there are anatomical advantages in the length of the Achilles tendon, the longest tendon in the body. I do not know the true reasons.' A typical reaction was that of the *Toronto Star*, which called Bannister 'a British upper class snot' and his remarks 'diabolical'. When reporters contacted the University of Toronto, not a single academic would dare pass comment. They instead issued a statement through an intermediary, citing their fear of 'jeopardizing one's own academic background'.

Black athletes themselves are not so squeamish. When Britain's former world champion hurdler Colin Jackson was asked why Britain's young athletes were so promising, he said, 'I think the colour of their skin might have something to do with it... It's obvious really.'[10] Carl Lewis agreed, stating simply that 'Blacks are made better.'[11] This is the Carl Lewis who won four gold medals at the 1984 Olympics by training for just eight hours a week.

But why should this be? According to Lee Evans, the African American civil rights campaigner who broke the 400 metres world record at the 1968 Olympics, the reason is that slavery functioned as a de facto eugenics programme.[12] Most slaves were taken from West Africa. Individuals were selected for size and strength so that they would be effective manual labourers. The weaker among them died on the journey from

Africa to the Americas due to the horrific conditions aboard slave ships. Whatever the merits of this theory, the fact remains that populations exhibit subtle differences in the constitution of their muscle tissue. West Africans have a preponderance of 'fast twitch' muscle fibres geared to produce bursts of power. However, this severely hampers their efforts in endurance events. East African leg muscles by contrast contain more 'slow twitch' fibres better suited to distance running than sprinting. In 2004, a team of researchers genetically engineered 'marathon mice' that could run twice as far as normal rodents by increasing the proportion of slow twitch muscle fibres in their limbs.[13]

Most striking of all is the success of athletes from the Kalenjin tribe in north-western Kenya. They represent 1/2000th of the world's population, yet since the eighties they have won 40 per cent of first-class international long-distance events. Half of these honours have gone to runners from the Nandi district alone, which is home to just 500,000 people (1/12,000th of the world's population). The Kalenjin live on a plateau 6,000 feet above sea level, which means that while they are growing up their bodies have to adapt to low concentrations of oxygen in the air. This increases their red blood cell count and cardiovascular capacity and gives them an enviable advantage when competing at lower altitudes. But this is not the crucial factor in their success, for Danish researchers have found that there is no difference between Kenyans' and Scandinavians' capacity to consume oxygen. Neither were Kenyan children found to spend more time running than their Danish counterparts. Where they differ is in the body shapes typical of their respective populations. The Kalenjin people boast an ideal physique for the sport, with long, thin legs and high calf muscles.

Compared to a Danish athlete of similar body mass, the average Kenyan runner has 400 grams less flesh in each lower leg, leaving his body weight closer to his centre of gravity and thereby easier to propel. To gauge how much difference this makes, consider that just 50 grams of extra weight on each ankle is enough to reduce oxygen efficiency by 1 per cent. Kenyan athletes can shrug off fatigue because they enjoy higher levels of an enzyme that breaks down lactate, and this therefore accumulates more slowly in their bodies. These characteristics mean that they can squeeze up to 10 per cent more energy than a European can out of the same volume of oxygen.[14] No surprise then that the Dane who finally managed to beat Sebastian Coe's sixteen-year-old world record in the 800 metres in 1997 was originally from Kenya. Wilson Kipketer, who ran the 800 metres in 1:41.24 in Zurich, was born into the Kalenjin tribe in Kapchemoiywo, and only later became a Danish citizen.

To some on the liberal left, acknowledging these facts puts us on a slippery slope of racial differences that leads inexorably to Auschwitz. They would rather pretend that they do not exist and instead explain the Kalenjins' success in terms of the sport's popularity in Kenya. Star runners become positive role models for young athletes, they claim, and as the protégés strive to emulate their heroes the cycle begins afresh. However, in Kenya and East Africa as a whole, football is even more popular than running, yet Kenya's national side has never qualified for the World Cup or even reached the second round of the African Nations Cup. East Africa has never produced a single soccer player worthy of note. West Africa, with a population better suited to 'power' sports, has produced dozens. As for the financial incentives given to Kenyan distance runners, there are also incentives on offer for success in sprinting. Unsurprisingly, the latter have so far been ineffective in re-engineering Kenyan physiognomy. Training makes existing muscle fibres bigger, but it cannot turn slow twitch fibres into fast twitch fibres or vice versa.

Liberal extremists would have us believe that Kenyans put more effort into their training than their rivals do (and, they insist, it is demeaning to the Kenyans to suggest that there is anything else to do with it). But, as Jon Entine writes: 'For their argument to prevail, one would have to believe that British and American blacks are hard-training sprinters but lazy distance runners.' Similarly, it would be absurd to suggest that Kenyans possess a will to win over the longer distances that evaporates when faced with short sprints. The liberal argument, while at odds with the evidence, is supposed to be morally preferable to the alternative. Now we can see that it is not even that. Delving into the physiological underpinnings of an athlete's success ought not to devalue their achievement. After all, there has to be *some* physiological basis to every athlete's success, no matter what his or her ethnicity.

Are sumo wrestlers fat but fit – or just plain fat?

In the early nineties, the Hawaiian-born wrestler Konishiki, 'The Dump Truck', became the first non-Japanese sumo champion – and a celebrity in the West. The heaviest sumo of all time, his weight peaked at 630 pounds (45 stone) and he is reputed to have once finished off 100 beers and seventy pieces of sushi in one sitting, yet he was still able to do the splits (intentionally). Most sumos, or *rikishi* as they are known, have a low fat ratio for their size, with a lot of hidden muscle, and can move gracefully around the ring. However, Konishiki was forced to retire at the age of 34 with arthritic knees and was soon unable to walk more than a few paces without suffering extreme pain.

For obvious reasons, knee problems are an occupational hazard for veteran sumo wrestlers, though matters are made worse because their training, and the preamble to each fight, involves stamping their feet. Injuries have increased in the sport as *rikishi* have become heavier in recent decades. Today, the average sumo wrestler eats between 5,000 and 10,000 calories a day, stands six feet tall, weighs 392 pounds (28 stone), will retire at the age of 31 and die at 56. To put that into context, the average Japanese man can expect to live to see 77. *Rikishi* may well have a lower body fat ratio than one would expect, and be surprisingly agile, but it's a curious kind of fitness that takes twenty years off one's life.

Wrestlers begin training at around the age of 14. Scouts look for unusually stout youngsters, but they must also be the fittest and strongest of their peers rather than simply the most overweight. However, fat soon becomes a fixation. Since there are no weight divisions in sumo, and contests can involve fighting someone twice your size, every *rikishi* must strive to pile on as many pounds as possible. Part of that will be muscle, but fat too helps to increase a wrestler's inertia, making him harder to manhandle out of the ring.

In order to bulk up, a typical exercise regime will consist of a five-hour training session on an empty stomach in the morning. At noon they eat their largest meal of the day: an enormous helping of *chankonabe* – a beef, chicken or fish and vegetable stew served with rice, often washed down with beer for extra calories. *Chankonabe* is a healthy meal in itself, but eaten in gargantuan quantities, followed by a four-hour nap to retain as much as possible in the body's fat stores, it becomes what Konishiki calls 'a sort of legal steroid'.[15] When they wake up it is time for another cauldron of *chankonabe*, more beer and some more sleep. Over the years, this way of eating steadily expands their stomach capacity.

Sumos may have a great deal of subcutaneous fat, but their huge frames harbour relatively little of the arterial or deep body fat that leads to heart attacks. This is because wrestlers take far more exercise than ordinary obese people. Unfortunately, many wrestlers carry on eating at the same pace after they retire, and it's then that the distribution of their body fat soon changes in dangerous ways. Diabetes – rare in practising sumos – becomes common in former wrestlers. High blood pressure becomes uncontrollable and coronary heart disease is a major threat.

In 1998, alarmed by the rising injury toll, Japan's sumo association ordered wrestlers to slim down. The call seems to have been heeded, though it's less popular with the fans and attendances at matches have declined. The current champion, Byamba, is a 6'1" Mongolian who weighs a 'mere' 340 pounds (24 stone). In 2006, a group of wrestlers even brought out a keep-fit DVD, *Sumo Health Exercises*, in which the 22-stone Hokutosho demonstrated squats and stretches to tempt teenagers into a healthy lifestyle 'instead of playing computer games all day'.[16] Needless to say, it also included instructions on how to make *chankonabe*.

Why do female tennis players grunt?

Maria Sharapova currently holds tennis's grunting record with a shriek measured at 101.2 decibels, which is comparable to a police car siren. She is so loud that at one pre-Wimbledon tournament in Birmingham, the players on a neighbouring court complained that they could not concentrate. Her trademark yelp is even available for download as a mobile phone ringtone. Despite objections from opponents, tennis fans and officials, she has no plans to change her habit. At press conferences, Sharapova has proudly worn a T-shirt bearing the slogan 'I feel pretty when I grunt'. On the strength of her results she should certainly carry on screaming: she was uncharacteristically quiet against Serena Williams in the final of the 2007 Australian Open, and went down accordingly in straight sets. She was also hushed when Justin Henin-Hardenne brought her nineteen-match winning run to an end in Madrid in November 2007.

A handful of male players have also grunted their way to victory, including Rafael Nadal, Jimmy Connors and Andre Agassi, though the latter once failed to defeat Ivan Lendl in the US Open despite being allowed to go on screaming the court down in the face of his opponent's protests. But it was only in 1992 that Monica Seles made the first steps towards making grunting an issue for tennis fans. Her 83 decibels – modest by today's standards – inspired *The Sun* newspaper to create the 'Gruntometer'. During that year's Wimbledon tournament, Jennifer Capriati is said to have shouted at Seles to 'Shut the fuck up!', while an exasperated Martina Navratilova complained that her opponent sounded 'like a stuck pig'. Finally, an umpire asked Seles to contain herself. Suitably warned, she lost in the final to Steffi Graf.

Action from the authorities has since been less conspicuous. When Wimbledon's chief referee Alan Mills retired in 2005, he complained that officials can only act if the offender is 'shown to be making the noises on purpose, which is virtually impossible to do', and called for a crackdown. But today, thanks to Seles, Sharapova and many others, grunting is so common that it rarely provokes comment, which is odd when spectators are ordered to be quiet so as not to distract the players. The non-grunters also seem to have given up protesting for fear of appearing to be bad losers – a chagrined Elena Dementieva explained: 'Next time I beat [Maria Sharapova] I may say something. But when you're losing 6-1, 4-1 it doesn't look good.'[17]

This is unfortunate, since grunting is clearly a form of gamesmanship even if for Sharapova it is not something done deliberately. It is rumoured that coaches are teaching players to use grunting as an integral part of their game, whether because it helps to focus aggression – rather like a martial artist breaking a plank – or because it intimidates one's opponent. Nick Bollettieri, the sport's most celebrated trainer, objects that 'Never once has that entered into my mind. But I believe releasing your energy is good because if you don't, it tightens up the body.'[18] The celebrated American varsity coach Bill Maze said that he had never taught grunting to his students, but argues, 'It's certainly strategic sometimes. The grunters seem to get louder when the point is bigger. These players are probably doing whatever they can to get an edge over their opponents.'[19]

The worst offenders insist that it is not a tactic to gain an advantage, but simply an involuntary release at a moment of exertion. However, cricketers and baseball players score sixes and home runs without bellowing, and high jumpers manage to clear the bar with shouting themselves over it. Even in tennis itself, Chris Evert and Billie Jean King played in silence, while Roger Federer, arguably the best player of all time, hits his hardest shots with barely a murmur. Martial arts enthusiasts may claim that shouting helps one to focus 'chi' energy when extra force is needed to break a brick, but unfortunately there is no such thing as chi energy as far as scientists are concerned. In fact, a study at Hardin-Simmons University in Texas in 1999 showed that grunting made no difference whatsoever to one's power in performing a dead lift.

As Martina Navratilova explained at the beginning of the dispute in 1992, there is more to grunting than merely irritating the opposition. The sound made by the strings of a racquet striking the ball gives the skilled player an important clue about the speed and spin of the ball they are about to face. Drowning this sound out with a loud grunt is obviously going to deny that information to your adversary. Even if grunting does help to add power to a smash, it's important to note that Sharapova shrieks even when she lobs the ball.

Is 'form' an illusion?

In the spring of 2006, a video clip from a high school basketball game in Rochester, New York became a sensation on the Internet. The star was Jason McElwain, an autistic boy who had worked as the assistant for his varsity team for three years, never missing a match. The coach had decided to reward McElwain's dedication by sending him on to the court in the last minutes of the last home game of the season, so long as the team held a comfortable lead. When Greece Athena duly moved twenty points ahead of Spencerport, McElwain's moment came and his mother prayed that her son be allowed to score 'just one point'. His first shot missed by six feet, but his well-meaning teammates made sure that he had another chance. This time he scored a three-pointer, the first of six within four minutes that tied the school record and sent Hollywood studios scrambling for the rights to his story. 'I was on fire,' he said afterwards, and all were agreed that for four minutes McElwain had entered the mythical state of mind and body known in sports as 'the Zone.'

In the Zone, everything feels and goes right for a player. As Purvis Short of the Golden State Warriors basketball team put it, 'You're in a world all your own. It's hard to describe. But the basket seems to be so wide. No matter what you do, you know the ball is going to go in.' From the spectator's point of view, the athlete in the Zone temporarily possesses what is referred to as a 'hot hand'. According to the 'hot hand' theory, success breeds success for sportsmen and -women. A string of goals or baskets means that a player will have a greater chance of succeeding in his or her subsequent attempt to score than would be suggested by his usual performance level. This is usually attributed to the increased confidence a player enjoys after a string of successes. He will be more relaxed when he attempts shots and will shoot from positions he would not have considered in the midst of a 'cold' run. According to one survey, 91 per cent of basketball fans believe that a player has a better chance of scoring if he has scored with his previous two or three shots. Commentators seem to concur, often remarking on a whether a player is 'hot' or 'cold', as do professional coaches and players themselves, who seek to get the ball to the player perceived to have the 'hot' hand as often as possible.

There is something obviously amiss with the notion of the hot hand from the outset, in that were it true that the probability of scoring increases with every success, then a player would never be less likely to miss than when he actually does miss. The probability of his success would increase indefinitely and we would expect him to reach an 'escape velocity' beyond which he will score with every touch. This of course never happens, and for reasons additional to a simple 'regression towards the mean' (the process whereby an unusually high or low level of performance is likely to be followed by a performance closer to the average for that individual). The more confident a player becomes, the more outlandish the shots he is willing to attempt and the more likely it is that he will fail. Defences also take notice and will take extra care to guard or mark that player. He then feels that his hand has gone 'cold', instead of drawing the obvious conclusion that he attempted a play that was beyond his talents.

A team of researchers analysed the games of the NBA's Philadelphia 76ers in the 1980–1 season and found that 'hot' streaks occurred no more often than would be predicted by pure chance.[20] A player who, over the course of the season, scores with 50 per cent of his attempts has a 50 per cent chance of scoring with any given shot whether or not he is riding on the back of several consecutive hits. However, we often think otherwise because we have a shaky grasp of probability. If one flips a coin a hundred times, the result will probably not be an even alternation of heads and tails. Although we can expect a roughly equal number of heads and tails overall, there will usually be significant clumps of one or the other at several stages. If the chance of scoring a basket is 50 per cent, then a string of five hits will occur around once in every thirty-two sequences. The better the player and the greater his base chance of scoring, the longer and more frequent those strings of hits will be.

The 76ers were in fact slightly *less* likely to score after making three baskets in a row. In interviews, the players claimed the opposite and cited the experience of 'the Zone', when after a string of hits they 'knew' that the next one would go in too. This just goes to show that good form is not a sensation. While in a confident mood, the 76ers tended to attempt more risky plays that predictably ended in failure. Their internal experience of the hot streak was nothing more than a judgment about their likelihood of scoring, and not a very accurate one as it turned out. The sensation itself was not an integral part of the scoring process. The feeling of empowerment did not translate into improved results, and the players' beliefs to the contrary were the product of a selective memory that recorded the successes but not the failures.

A player cannot argue with the numbers no matter how strongly he feels, and the research in question has been repeated many times in a voluminous literature on the subject, and not just in basketball. For example, a study of thirty-five professional golfers on the 1997 PGA Tour showed that they were just as likely to birdie a hole following a par or worse than following a birdie or better.[21] Yet even in horse racing, where the result is far more down to the horse than its rider, jockeys are often thought to be on hot streaks. The following advice is from a Raceform manual published in 1987:

> Follow the man in form is a particularly apt adage when
> it comes to jockeys. So often everything seems to go
> right with those who are enjoying a successful run. A
> string of winners gives most jockeys added confidence;
> and attempts at difficult tactics and daring manoeuvres
> have a habit of coming off for those riding on the crest
> of a wave... Those who are out of luck seem to stay out
> of luck, losing dash and confidence and failing on horses
> on which they should have won.[22]

Unfortunately, this is one of those rare pieces of nonsense that gains in truth the more people believe in it. The author eventually hits the nail on the head when he continues: 'Moreover, the men in form get the best mounts, as owners and trainers tend to overlook jockeys who are not currently riding winners.' This is entrenched by the common practice of big-name jockeys bumping smaller names off the race card when they fancy their chances on a particular mount scheduled for someone else.

It is really the fans' and pundits' emotions that are at issue, because it is they who read too much meaning into statistical clumps. As the political scientist David Runciman has pointed out, in England this irrationality manifests itself in the Premiership's Manager of the Month competition, which is won by whoever has been lucky enough to preside over an unlikely string of four or five victories. When that team then loses its next game, fans evince surprise and invoke the so-called 'Curse of the Manager of the Month'. 'It's not inevitable that they should lose their next game, of course,' writes Runciman. 'The Manager of the Month wins some and loses some. It's just that we remember the losses, and dress them up into a curse, because we can't distinguish between statistically meaningless sequences and the march of destiny.'[23] The urge to impute meaning into sequences is so strong that organizers of the multiple-choice SAT tests in the United States ensure that long runs of the same letter never occur. They fear that students will believe such strings to be unlikely and, doubting their own correct answers, might choose a wrong letter to break the run.

Sport remains steeped in talk of 'form' despite the refutation of the concept in the nineties. Players are sometimes 'in form' and sometimes 'out of form', while certain individuals are particularly streaky and blow hot and cold throughout the season, lighting up certain matches and fading away in others. There are various explanations for the phenomenon: some sportsmen are said to be 'confidence players' who can only produce the goods when they are inspired to believe in themselves by a kindly manager prepared to give them an extended run in the team; others are lazy so-and-sos who earn so much money that they cannot be bothered to make the effort in every game. There is nothing wrong with describing a player as being 'in form' if all that means is that he is enjoying a period of greater than average success given his ability. But we should not imagine that there must always be a special reason for this success, still less that such a player should quickly be picked for the national side before his form evaporates. If one were to take fifty coins and flip each one twenty times, we could expect a few to fall on heads several times in a row, followed by a string of tails. Yet we would not want to say that these coins are 'in form' or 'confident' during unbroken stretches of heads. Neither would we describe those coins that exhibit alternating runs of four heads and four tails as 'lazier' than coins that exhibit a more haphazard distribution.

People, of course, are not quite like coins. They are not mechanical or circumscribed; they are capricious, open-ended creatures. Presumably, some players *are* lazy, and there may be many reasons beyond pure chance for a player's sudden improvement or loss of form. He might have employed a new trainer, gained or lost weight, suffered a family tragedy or begun to use newly designed equipment. He may also have started to use performance-enhancing drugs or shaken off a niggling injury. Any theory that dismisses such 'rigged' streaks as explicable by chance must clearly be mistaken. But if these extra factors are telling, then we should be able to correlate periods of form with their involvement. When we cannot, the maths takes over and the much-vaunted 'Zone' has no more reality than Camelot.

Do gloves make boxing more dangerous?

Promotional posters for boxing matches in the nineteenth century followed a formula: the two adversaries would be depicted squaring up to each other, with heads tilted slightly backwards and their fists held low, the knuckles pointing out and upwards. The pose looks comical today, as if they are actors in a silent movie rather than pugilists. The stance and guard were low because bare-knuckle boxing consisted largely of striking the opponent's body. The skull is an extremely hard object, and a full-force punch to an opponent's head could easily result in a broken hand. This is why so many bar-room brawls end after one punch. The 'boxer's fracture' – a break behind the knuckle of the little finger – is regularly seen in hospital casualty departments at the weekend.

The Marquis of Queensbury's rules took off not because society viewed the new sport as more civilized than the old, but because fights conducted under the new guidelines attracted more spectators. Audiences wanted to see repeated blows to the head and dramatic knockouts. By contrast, the last bare-knuckle heavyweight contest in the US in 1897 dragged on into the seventy-fifth round. Since gloves spread the impact of a blow, the recipient of a punch is less likely to be blinded, have their teeth knocked out or their jaw broken. However, gloves do not lessen the force applied to the brain as it rattles inside the skull from a heavy blow. In fact, they make matters worse by adding ten ounces to the weight of the fist.

A full-force punch to the head is comparable to being hit with a twelve-pound padded wooden mallet travelling at 20 mph. Gerald McClellan took around forty such blows over the course of his world title fight against Nigel Benn in 1995. Even the most hardened spectators were shocked by its brutality. Neither fighter made any great attempts to defend himself. Instead, the two stood toe to toe, trading punches. This was boxing as the *Rocky* movies portrayed it, rather than the more tentative real-life affair of jabbing, circling and clinching. As a result, McClellan suffered brain damage that left him blind, 80 per cent deaf and paralysed.

As the bare-knuckle campaigner Dr Alan J. Ryan pointed out, 'In 100 years of bare-knuckle fighting in the United States, which terminated around 1897 with a John L. Sullivan heavyweight championship fight, there wasn't a single ring fatality. In 150 years of bare-knuckle fighting in England, prior to the introduction of the rules of the Marquis of Queensbury around 1885, there were only two fatalities.'[24] Today there are three or four every year in the US, and around 15 per cent of professional fighters suffer some form of permanent brain damage during their career. Worldwide there have been over four hundred boxing deaths in the last fifty years alone. The total would be far higher were it not for the advances in medical care that saved the lives of fighters such as McClellan and Michael Watson. A return to bare knuckles would be bloodier and less acceptable to mass television audiences, but one has to ask whether wheelchairs and life-support machines are any easier on one's conscience.

Could a human pyramid in the goalmouth defend a 1-0 lead?

Imagine that in the dying seconds of injury time at the Euro 2008 Final, the scoreline between England and Portugal stands at nil-nil. Aaron Lennon begins England's last attack with a high ball lofted into the Portuguese box as Peter Crouch makes his run. Crouch has been planning for this moment for two years, and he puts his weight training to good use as he picks Michael Owen up by the waist and lifts his strike partner clear of the opposing defence. Owen heads the winning goal of the competition with ease, and the linesman is altogether too startled to raise his flag. Wearing their victors' medals, the pair repeat their stunt for the photographers at the hoisting of the cup, and a new dance craze leads to broken collarbones across the nation...

Well, why not? At first sight, there appears to be nothing in the rules of football against picking up a teammate, just as there is nothing in the rules of rugby union against giving another player an 'assist' during a line-out. But, according to the Professional Game Match Officials organization, Peter Crouch should receive a yellow card for 'ungentlemanly conduct' from the referee. There are many similar wheezes that sportsmen and -women never attempt despite the urging of lay observers at big tournaments. Sometimes the rulebook brings a swift end to the discussion. Why can't a player's teammates link arms and form a barrier around him as he dribbles towards goal? Because obstructing opponents is not allowed. Why can't a tennis player 'catch' a lobbed ball on his racquet, then stroll up to the net and drop it over the other side? Because that would be construed as hitting the ball twice, which again is not allowed. But more often than not, the reason why there is no law against a manoeuvre is that there is no need for one – because it cannot be done.

Consider the practicality of Crouch and Owen's last-minute goal. In rugby, players are allowed to handle the ball, which is thrown carefully from a short distance away. Footballers, by contrast, typically have to cover more ground to connect with a cross, and the problem is that neither the lifter nor the liftee will be especially mobile in this arrangement. Faced with a jostling defence and a fast-moving ball played in from the wing, Crouch and Owen would be more likely to topple over and add to the injury list than make successful contact with the ball.

But what of the favourite question asked by the uninitiated when a football team surrenders a 1-0 lead in the ninetieth minute: why on earth didn't they just form a human pyramid covering their goalmouth? The fact is that you would need more than eleven players to form a big enough pyramid. With half the team standing on the other half's shoulders, most of the target would be undefended, so they would have to position themselves side by side. According to FA regulations, the goalposts must be 7.32 metres (8 yards) apart, measured from their inner edges. Assuming that each player in the 'shield wall' covers 50 cm, that still leaves almost two metres of space to shoot at from close range, not counting mishaps and nutmegs through their legs.

A larger player like Bill 'Fatty' Foulke, the 24-stone giant who kept goal for Sheffield United, Chelsea, Bradford and England in the 1890s and 1900s, might stretch more generously to, say, 75 cm. An entire team composed of such behemoths might almost have the width covered, but one doubts whether they would have much luck jumping to head away the high balls. The crossbar must be 2.44 metres (8 feet) from the ground, and as Fatty stands 191 cm in his studs, that still leaves a slot of over half a metre above his head. Perhaps the team could make up the deficit by taking to the field with afro hairstyles heavily gelled into shot-stopping hardness, but none of this would help their chances of going 1-0 up in the first place. Neither could they hope to play for a scoreless draw. They would soon buckle under the hail of shots, some destined for their faces and groins, while the inevitable handballs would lead to penalty kicks. The tactic would, of course, render the offside rule useless for the defending team, so shots could be taken from point-blank range. Eventually, someone would have the far better idea of hoofing the ball up the field.

Have the Olympic Games ever made a profit?

After Montreal won the bidding to host the 1976 Olympic Games, Mayor Jean Drapeau said: 'The Olympics can no more lose money than a man can have a baby.' Costs were estimated initially at US$310 million, and Monsieur Drapeau was confident that the public finances would turn a significant profit. But due to irresponsible management, industrial action, political corruption and an increase in security costs after terrorism disrupted the 1972 Munich Games, the bill escalated to over US$2 billion. Taxpayers only managed to pay off the final instalment in December 2006, thirty years after an event that lasted only two weeks. The Canadians did not win even a single gold medal for their trouble.

History seemed to be repeating itself in 2007, when London's Mayor Ken Livingstone promised that the latest increase in the bill for the 2012 Games would only cost each household 'less than the price of a Walnut Whip every week'. On the other side of the Atlantic, Patrick Ryan, the leader of Chicago's bid for the 2016 Games, was insisting that every summer Olympics in the last three decades had made a profit. He tried to allay local taxpayers' fears by projecting a $525 million surplus and joking that to make a loss 'we would have to be the first really incompetents'.[25] The latter prediction would seem to be the strongest based on Mr Ryan's grasp of the figures. He had looked only at the budgets of local organizing committees and ignored the costs of building new infrastructure.

It was spending on infrastructure for the 2004 Games that sank the taxpayers of Athens by devouring 5 per cent of the entire nation's GDP. Many of the specially built venues have lain empty since the closing ceremony, among them a $144 million sailing facility, yet together they require $100 million a year to be spent on their upkeep. Serafim Kotrotsos, the head of communications for the organizing committee, explained: 'It's like we built a brand new house, held a great party, then closed it and now have no guests.'[26] Expenditure on the Games quadrupled from the original estimate to almost £9 billion ($18 billion), resulting in a 6 per cent budget deficit for Greece, which thereby breached the Eurozone's economic stability pact. The Sydney Games of 2000 only overran by £75 million ($150 million) on an initial £1.4 billion ($2.8billion), but this figure will be rising into the future with the multi-million-pound cost of maintaining dozens of white elephants. These include the £200 million ($400 million) Olympic Stadium itself, which remains heavily in debt and is usually silent. As New South Wales assemblyman Chris Hartcher put it, 'It is now clear that the post-Olympic plan was largely rhetoric. The huge capital investment in the Olympics will leave state finances haemorrhaging for years to come.'[27] Neither have Greece or Australia enjoyed a sustained increase in tourism resulting from the Games.

Bidding teams seem to make a habit of underestimating costs. For example, Atlanta's technology budget in 1996 was $10 million, but the final bill came to $400 million. This seems to have been simple human error – those responsible had taken their original figure from Barcelona's projection for the 1992 event, which itself turned out to be wildly inaccurate. Other instances have involved more cynical motives. As the German sports economist Holger Preuss explained, 'During the bidding competition, you need to convince the IOC and your population that the bid is a good thing, so you cannot make it too expensive. After you win, you adjust.'[28]

London's team has been adjusting furiously since 2005 when they won the right to host the 2012 Games. Tessa Jowell, the government minister responsible, was confident at the time that £2.375 billion ($4.74 billion) was a realistic costing. Two years later, she was forced to admit that the final bill would be closer to £9.35 billion. Only £2.2 billion of this will come from private investment. A fifth of the National Lottery budget for good causes up until 2013 has been sequestered to make up the shortfall, and arts funding across the country has already been cut by a third. This is after London's council tax payers have already been tapped for £625 million. In 2006, Ms Jowell announced a somewhat creative solution to the problem of the budget overrun: a group of consultants would be charged with ensuring that costs did not rise further and that the infrastructure would be built on schedule. For performing this service, CLM will be paid an additional £400 million not included in the original budget estimate. As London Assembly member Philip Davies said at the time, 'You couldn't make this up.' In November 2006, CLM were already behind schedule. The most popular explanation for the debacle among cynics and supporters alike is that the original estimate was not rigorous because it did not have to be, as no one thought that London's bid had a chance of winning.

The only Games in recent decades to boast a clear profit were Los Angeles in 1984 and Atlanta in 1996. LA cleared $200 million, partly from successful corporate sponsorship, but largely because, like Atlanta, the authorities built virtually nothing to order. Instead, events were hosted in existing venues and athletes were billeted in student halls. The 1948 London Games made a profit of £10,000 after competitors were housed in army and RAF camps in lieu of an Olympic village. History thus proves that a profitable Olympics is possible, so long as the organizers do not do anything as rash as constructing an entire town for the purpose. Unfortunately, this is precisely what the 2012 team plans to do.

According to *Private Eye* magazine, the March 2007 estimate for the price of the 2012 Games means that it will cost more to stage than the annual gross domestic product of the following (sixty-six) competing countries: Albania, Antigua and Barbuda, Armenia, the Bahamas, Bahrain, Barbados, Belize, Benin, Bhutan, Botswana, Brunei Darussalam, Burkina Faso, Burundi, Cape Verde, Central African Republic, Chad, Comoros, Republic of Congo, Djibouti, Dominica, Eritrea, Fiji, Gabon, the Gambia, Georgia, Grenada, Guinea-Bissau, Guyana, Haiti, Iceland, Jamaica, Kiribati, Kyrgyz Republic, Laos, Lesotho, Liberia, Macedonia, Madagascar, Malawi, Maldives, Mali, Malta, Mauritania, Mauritius, Moldova, Mongolia, Namibia, Netherlands Antilles, Niger, Papua New Guinea, Rwanda, Samoa, São Tomé and Principe, Seychelles, Sierra Leone, Solomon Islands, St Kitts and Nevis, St Lucia, St Vincent and Grenadines, Suriname, Swaziland, Tajikistan, Timor-Leste, Togo, Tonga, Vanuatu and Zambia.[29]

How does reverse swing work?

According to one of its greatest exponents, the Pakistani all-rounder Imran Khan, the phenomenon of reverse swing is too complex for ordinary minds to grasp. In fact, those who have not benefited from a first-rate education are apt to mistake it for a form of cheating. As he told *India Today* magazine in June 1994, 'Look at people who have taken a rational stand on this. Tony Lewis, Christopher Martin-Jenkins, Derek Pringle. They are educated Oxbridge types. Look at the others: Lamb, Botham and Trueman. Class and upbringing makes a difference.' Botham's response was: 'If an Oxford education tells you that it's alright to cheat, then give me Buckler's Mead Secondary Modern School any time.'[30]

So what is reverse swing? And why is it so contentious? Conventional swing is when the ball moves sideways in the air as it approaches the batsman, in the direction the seam is pointing. As one would expect, reverse swing is when the ball moves away from the seam instead. Reverse swing may have been achieved by accident early in cricket's history, but it was Pakistan's Sarfraz Nawaz who first employed it by design. In 1979, he bewildered Australia's batting order in the Melbourne Test, taking nine wickets in one innings, including a spell of seven wickets for just one run. His technique reached the popular consciousness when it was used by his countrymen

Waqar Younis and Wasim Akram to torment England in the summer of 1992. Because English bowlers could not replicate what they were seeing, it was thought that the Pakistani tourists must be breaking the rules somehow. However, it is not necessary to understand the theory behind reverse swing in order to put it into practice. This is just as well, because only fairly recently has anyone been able to provide a properly authoritative account of how it works. Several bogus explanations have gathered momentum over the years, including putting the effect down to humidity or to one hemisphere of the ball becoming wet and therefore heavier.

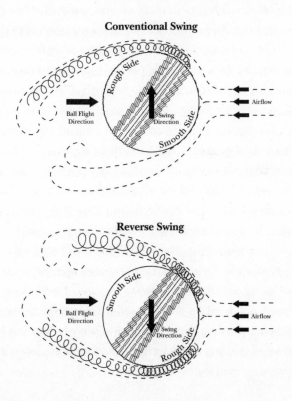

Conventional Swing

Rough Side

Ball Flight Direction

Swing Direction

Smooth Side

Airflow

Reverse Swing

Smooth Side

Ball Flight Direction

Swing Direction

Rough Side

Airflow

Conventional swing was investigated in a 1983 paper in *Nature*, science's most prestigious journal.[31] A team led by Rabindra Mehta, a professor of aerodynamics and school friend of Imran Khan's, found that for optimum swing the ball should be delivered at 35–70 mph with the seam angled at 20 degrees and with a backspin of eleven revolutions per second. Swing is produced by a difference in air pressure between the left and right sides of the ball. As the ball travels forwards, a thin 'boundary layer' of air forms at its leading face, flows around its sides and eventually separates in the way that water will flow around a rock in a stream. The layer will separate early if the surface of the ball is very smooth, allowing a smooth flow of air. However, if the seam is off-centre from the direction of the ball's flight, then the leading edge will trip the boundary layer on that side into a turbulent state, which allows it to cling to the ball for longer. This means that this side will be subject to lower air pressure, thereby pushing the ball in that direction.

The leading hemisphere should be kept as smooth as possible to ensure an even, rapid flow of air on that side. Methods of maintaining the required sheen have been legion. Only sweat and saliva may be applied to the ball legally, but the use of many other substances has been alleged and sometimes proven. Lip balm and Brylcreem are the usual suspects. India's Rahul Dravid forfeited half his match fee after he was spotted rubbing a throat lozenge on a ball during a one-day game against Zimbabwe in 2004. During the 2005 Ashes series, England were rumoured to have used 'magic mints' that infused their saliva with sugar to give it better polishing properties. It was never proven, but Mike Selvey joked that 'it is a wonder that a number of England players still have their own teeth'.[32]

Different rules apply at speeds over 70 mph, as the boundary layer on the smooth side also starts to become turbulent, reducing the pressure differential between the two sides. Eighty mph is a dead zone for swing. England's Matthew Hoggard produces swing reliably by bowling at 80 mph or thereabouts, but the ball has slowed to 70–75 mph by the time it pitches, thereby swinging late. But at speeds greater than 85 mph, the ball can suddenly swing the 'wrong' way. Professor Mehta was sceptical of such reports at first, but his experiments subsequently showed that at very high speeds the boundary

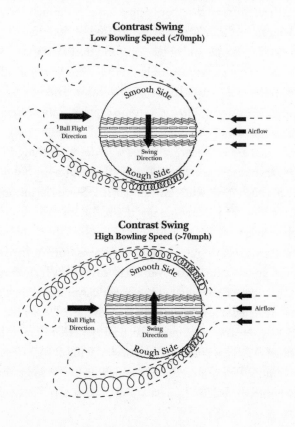

layer becomes turbulent before it even gets to the seam.[33] However, when it does, the seam actually reduces the effect of the turbulence on that side by causing the boundary layer to break away sooner than it does on the smooth side of the ball. Swing is thereby reversed. Very few bowlers are capable of delivering the ball at over 85 mph, but lesser arms can also achieve a degree of reverse swing if they lead with the rough side of the ball. The rougher the surface, the lower the speed required to produce swing.

Although the condition of a ball deteriorates the longer it is used, the process does not happen quickly enough for most bowlers. Younis and Wasim were accused of 'gouging' the ball with long fingernails and bottle tops, and the Pakistan team has been dogged by allegations of ball-tampering ever since. They are not the only suspects. In a pre-season friendly against Nottinghamshire in 2007, the Kent captain Robert Key was even caught using sandpaper on the ball, though it was not an ECB fixture so technically he was doing nothing illegal. Fielders can return a ball to the wicketkeeper on the bounce in order to rough it up, while bowlers such as Steve Harmison and Andrew Flintoff naturally bang the ball hard into the pitch, which speeds wear and tear. All this has enabled the best bowlers to start reverse swinging the ball as early as the fifteenth over (Younis and Wasim took over forty overs). In fact, there is nothing to stop it swinging in its very first over, since roughness can be created not just by picking pieces of the ball away, but also by sticking dirt to it, though one wonders whether Imran Khan's 'educated Oxbridge types' would be as forgiving of such unsubtle behaviour. When Mike Atherton appeared to rub soil from his pocket onto the ball in the Test against South Africa at Lords in

1994, Ray Illingworth fined him £2,000, and even the public-school-educated Jonathan Agnew called for the England captain's resignation.

In preparation for their Ashes revenge against England, Australia's bowling coach Troy Cooley went one better than Oxbridge and consulted NASA. Rabindra Mehta returned to analyse and replicate a newly discovered form of swing in the US space agency's wind tunnels. When Bob Woolmer identified what he called 'converse' swing in August 2006, many commentators rolled their eyes, with one authority remarking, 'The theory makes no sense to me... I think it is simply Woolmer looking for some attention again.'[34] Converse or 'contrast' swing is when a bowler swings the ball conventionally with one delivery and, with the same grip and ball condition, reverse swings it the next. Professor Mehta found that it is no myth. The ball needs to be delivered with the seam aligned in the direction of flight rather than at an angle and one side needs to be rough. At speeds lower than 70 mph, the air in the boundary layer on the rough side becomes turbulent and the ball swings in that direction. Faster than that and both sides become turbulent, but the layer of turbulent air on the rough side will be thicker and weaker, so the ball will swing in the direction of the smooth side.

Imran Khan was right that reverse swing required an educated mind to comprehend, but it was one that outstripped even his own. As for his claim that upbringing was also necessary, by the time of the 2005 Ashes series, Britain's school standards had improved to the point where even a product of a comprehensive like Simon Jones could reverse swing the ball as well as any toff.

Can women ever compete with men in sport?

On 20 September 1973, the Houston Astrodome hosted one of the most anticipated tennis matches of all time. It began like no ordinary game. Twenty-nine-year-old Billy Jean King entered the court on a litter borne by four muscle-bound athletes dressed as ancient slaves. Her opponent, Bobby Riggs, arrived in a chariot drawn by young models in skin-tight outfits. This was the so-called 'Battle of the Sexes' between the world's greatest female player and a self-confessed 'male chauvinist pig'. The prize was $100,000 and bragging rights for the winner – Riggs declared that he wanted to be the 'number one pig'. King won in straight sets, 6-4, 6-3, 6-3. Her victory boosted the women's liberation movement and kicked off the growth in women's tennis that culminated in the recent decision to award equal prize money to the male and female Wimbledon champions.

As historically important as the contest was, there is no denying it was something of a mismatch. King was at the peak of her imperious powers, while Riggs was a 55-year-old has-been – only the third best player on the veterans' circuit by one account – who was showing early signs of a paunch and man boobs. He had last been at the top of his game thirty-four years earlier, when he won the 1939 Wimbledon tournament. Needless to say, considering Riggs managed to win ten games, the contest could hardly be called a victory for militant feminism. Almost twenty years later, the Battle of the Sexes was reprised for an audience at Caesars Palace, Las Vegas – and with a very different result. Forty-year-old Jimmy Connors beat 35-year-old Martina Navratilova 7-5, 6-2 despite being allowed only one serve and having to cover the width of the doubles court while his opponent kept to the singles lines.

Before that match it was a fairly common opinion among laypeople that Navratilova was good enough to compete with men, but this was far from the truth – and the same applies to claims made for other outstanding female sports stars. Since Michelle Wie's much hyped entry into men's golf competitions in 2005 she has not yet made the cut in a single tournament on the PGA tour – once missing out by fourteen shots. At the more modest Casio Open in Japan in 2006, she finished 101st out of 102 competitors. Her stated ambition to win the US Masters is looking like pure fantasy. And while some said American sprinter Florence Griffith Joyner was 'faster than most men', that only meant men who are not professional athletes. Flo Jo set a world record of 10.49 seconds in 1988. This is slower than the 10.4 recorded by Charlie Paddock in 1921, but Joyner would have beaten Paddock's 10.8 when he won Olympic gold in Antwerp in 1920. She would also have beaten the men in the 1912 Olympics in Stockholm, when Don Lippincott completed the dash in a time of 10.6 seconds. Given the circumstances of her early death, there are strong suspicions that Flo Jo's time was drug assisted. But chemically enhanced or not, the fact remains that 10.49 would currently only equal the second fastest time set by a British under-17-year-old schoolboy.

Female times on the track have been improving at a

greater rate than men's over the last 100 years. If the trend continues, according to research published in *Nature*, the fastest 100 metres sprint champion at the 2156 Olympics will be a woman. Her time will be 8.079 seconds, beating her male counterpart's time of 8.098.[35] This is unlikely, of course, since men are physically bigger and stronger than women. Instead, we can expect female athletes to hit their performance ceiling before male runners. The faster improvements that women have made are probably partially down to their exclusion from many sports until relatively recently. For example, there were no women in the Olympic marathon until 1984.

With the most politically correct will in the world, there are basic differences between male and female physiology that are pertinent to sporting aptitude. Aside from the obvious advantages of size and strength that mean that Michelle Wie will never be able to send a drive as far as the best male golfers, men have narrower pelvises and longer Achilles tendons to aid running speed. In similar sized individuals they have around 10 per cent less body fat, 10 per cent greater cardiovascular performance, larger hearts, more haemoglobin in the blood and much higher levels of the hormone testosterone that enhances muscle building and recovery time. However, in certain circumstances, it is their biological differences that enable women to finish on top.

Women's natural body fat gives them a built-in buoyancy aid that is very helpful in long-distance swimming. In chilly outdoor waters a layer of fat also reduces heat loss, with the result that several records in various long-distance events have been broken by women. Penny Lee Dean's record for swimming the English Channel stood for eighteen years. Around the world today, swimming honours are roughly even between men and women. Women's fat stores also enable them to compete with men in ultramarathons – races of typically 100 miles or 100 kilometres – where they enjoy the added advantage of high levels of oestrogen in their bloodstream that allows prolonged muscle function. The third event in which women can outperform men is in holding one's breath under extreme pressure. Britain's Tanya Streeter holds the world freediving record, having descended to a depth of 525 feet.

These exceptions are scarce and may only prove the rule that, in general, women cannot compete with men on the sports field. But not all sports require physical prowess. There would seem to be no reason why women should not do as well as men at indoor games such as snooker and darts or in shooting or car racing. Women have very rarely excelled in these to date, with the first two remaining uncharted territory. In 2005, Danica Patrick finished fourth in the Indianapolis 500 after leading for several laps – the best ever showing by a female competitor. But at the 1967 Pan-American Games, Margaret Murdock from Kansas broke the world record score for both sexes on her way to winning gold in small-bore rifle shooting. She then won silver in the 1976 Olympic Games, narrowly missing out on gold due to a judges' decision after a tie for first place. So why have there been so few women like Murdock?

According to one theory, men are simply more competitive than women due to their higher testosterone levels. There is also some evidence that sportswomen do not cope with pressure as well as the men. Professor Daniele Paserman of Hebrew University made a statistical study of the play during the 2006 US Open, French Open and Wimbledon tennis tournaments. He found that men made unforced errors on around 30 per cent of points across the board. The chance of error was no greater when they faced a crucial match or set point than when they were 5-0 up or down and the set was as good as decided already. However, Paserman also found that while women made unforced errors 34 per cent of the time on relatively unimportant points, this rose to 40 per cent on the most important.[36] The research is not conclusive, since it is not exactly comparing like with like. The truth may be to do less with concentration than participation. When it comes to the sports they would have a chance in, such as snooker and darts, women simply do not care enough to take a serious interest.

In motor racing, is the car or the driver more important?

'Driving skill hardly matters anymore,' complained legendary driver Juan Manuel Fangio in 1983. 'Today it is 95 per cent car. It is simple to prove. A driver can emerge in a good car, become World Champion and a year later disappear completely to the back of the grid.'[37] This works both ways. In the eighties and nineties, Keke Rosberg, Nigel Mansell and Damon Hill all posted mediocre results in Formula One with Fittipaldi, Lotus and Brabham respectively, yet they became champions when they switched to Williams. Hill swiftly found himself at the back of the grid again when he left Williams for the Arrows team, recording only a single podium finish in the season after he won the drivers' title. So was the skill of the driver paramount back in the Golden Age of motor racing? Not at all: 'In my day,' Fangio added, 'it was 75 per cent car and mechanics, 25 per cent driver and luck.' It should not have been even that much. In Fangio's era, many drivers were amateurs who should not have been on the same track as the great man. Today, however, there is relatively little to separate the way the top professionals handle a vehicle. Little, but not nothing.

The worst driver in the best car will do far better than the best driver in the worst car. According to Fernando Alonso himself, forget the car – the *tyres* are more important than the driver. In July 2006 he remarked, 'We have fantastic tyres on the car and Michelin are giving us the extra performance, that's why we are leading the championship.'[38] Renault's executive director of engineering, Pat Symonds, added that 'If you consider the five primary factors in the performance equation – engine, chassis, tyres, driver and team – the tyres account for at least 30 per cent of the performance package. A bigger separate percentage than any of the other factors, for sure.'[39] Well-designed tyres can bestow an advantage of half a second a lap. To achieve as much through increased engine power would require a boost of over 100 horsepower – several times what manufacturers expect to accomplish when they re-engineer a car.

But this does not mean that the skill of the driver goes unrecognized, or that race results give a largely deceitful account of the drivers' relative merits, because the best drivers tend to end up in the best cars for obvious reasons. If the drivers were not extremely important then teams would not pay them so much (Ferrari pay Kimi Raikkonen £23 million a year). One way to see what value teams are getting would be to examine the results achieved by Formula One drivers when they race in single-make series. From 1996, Formula 3000 used standardized cars for every team. Unfortunately, few of the currently active Formula One drivers raced against each other in Formula 3000. Nick Heidfeld finished the 1999 Formula 3000 season on 59 points – 29 ahead of his nearest rival. But in his first season in Formula One with the Prost team in 2000, he was forced to retire on ten occasions and failed to record a single point in the drivers' championship. His teammate Jean Alesi was similarly unsuccessful, with twelve retirements and no points. Of the Formula 3000 champions since 1996, only Juan

Pablo Montoya has won a Formula One Grand Prix.

This leaves us with comparing the success of drivers on the same teams. In terms of qualifying lap times, there tends to be a greater difference between the performance of teams than that of drivers on the same team. In the final standings in the drivers' leader board, team partners usually finish within three places of one another. Arguably, this is not close enough. In 2006, Fernando Alonso in a Renault won the championship by 13 points. But Renault's number two driver Giancarlo Fisichella could only manage to come fourth, recording only one win compared to the Ferrari-driving Michael Schumacher's seven. In 2005, Fisichella finished fifth, again with only one win. In the seventeen seasons between 1990 and 2006, a constructor has achieved first and second place in the drivers' championship on only four occasions. Even in 1992, when Nigel Mansell cruised to victory in an 'invincible' Williams with 108 points to his nearest rival's 56, his teammate Riccardo Patrese only held second place by three points to Michael Schumacher in third.

There are around 400 people in each Formula One team and only two drivers, but mechanics will say that the driver is the easiest part of the car to fix. Adding horsepower, for example, requires expensive and time-consuming research and development, whereas one driver can simply be swapped for another. But this ignores the role the driver plays in developing the machine, which to an extent is built around him. Drivers undertake thousands of kilometres of testing to give feedback on the car's performance. According to François Duforez, the director of France's Institut Biomédical Sport et Vie, physical conditioning is crucial: 'For a driver who is less strong physically, after a certain time his line will start to widen, he will commit an error here, an error there, and that will make him lose time.'[40]

It was Ayrton Senna and Nigel Mansell who started the trend for drivers to treat their bodies like those of athletes. Not a moment too soon either – going round a 5 G corner wearing a twelve-pound helmet feels like having a sixty-pound weight tied to one's head. Excellent reaction times and peripheral vision are equally important. Duforez also believes that these times can be too fast and that the optimum level is one that does not cause the overreaction that can lead to accidents. Finally, drivers need the strength of character to overcome the stress of the season and the inevitable bouts of bad luck.

In 2006, the Fédération Internationale de l'Automobile (FIA) surveyed 91,000 Formula One fans from 180 countries and found that 88 per cent wanted more emphasis on the skill of the driver and a cutback on technological crutches. Yet 91 per cent agreed that technology was an important driving force. If cars had to be identical, investment would dry up and the sport might lose its appeal. This does not mean that certain driver aids should not be outlawed, which is the fate that awaits traction control in 2008.

Three-time world champion Niki Lauda once said that with traction control allowing perfect full-throttle acceleration and steering-wheel paddles providing assisted gear changes, cars had become so computerized that a monkey could drive one. 'It is unbelievable compared to my time,' he scoffed. 'To operate the car in Monte Carlo we had to change gears about two thousand times. You had blisters in your hands. If you missed a gear once you would blow up your engine and lose the race.'[41] While Lauda was head of the Jaguar team in 2002, his drivers Eddie Irvine and Pedro de la Rosa challenged him to test-drive the car on Spain's Valencia circuit. To his embarrassment, he spun off twice during his first three laps.

Is marathon running bad for your health?

On 20 July 1984, the reputation of long-distance running suffered an embarrassing blow when Jim Fixx died at the age of 52 from a heart attack while jogging. Fixx was the pre-eminent guru of the sport's life-giving properties and author of the bestseller *The Complete Book of Running*. At the same time on the other side of the Atlantic, Jeanne Calment was finishing off the last of the two pounds of chocolate she ate every week and lighting up another cigarette. She had been smoking daily for ninety years and would do so for another eight before eventually expiring at a world record-breaking 122 years and 164 days. For one brief moment, the smugness of couch potatoes and chain smokers exceeded that of keep-fit fanatics.

However, the full story is not so salutary. Madame Calment had lived a highly active life. She had been an enthusiastic swimmer and tennis player and continued to ride her bicycle past her centenary year. Her cigarette intake was less than one pack a week. The unfortunate Jim Fixx, on the other hand, had been overweight for much of his life and smoked forty a day until he was 35. His autopsy revealed that the three arteries supplying blood to his heart muscle were clogged so badly that it was a wonder he had lasted as long as he had. Coronary heart disease ran in the family, but at least he outlived his father, who died of a cardiac arrest at 43.

Sceptics have been critical of vigorous exercise for thousands of years, ever since the experience of the man who started it all off – Pheidippides the Greek, who promptly dropped dead from exhaustion after reaching his destination and announcing victory over the Persians at the Battle of Marathon in 490 BC. But in his case we are talking of slightly more than the standard 26 miles 385 yards (42.195 km), as according to legend he had not yet recovered from running 150 miles in two days to seek the aid of Sparta. Long-distance running was thought to be so debilitating for the fairer sex that there was no women's marathon event at the Olympics until 1984.

It was once believed that every heart had a certain number of beats within it, and when they had been used up that was the end of you. So it made sense to ensure that your heart did not spend much of its time racing away. But we now know that a healthy heart beats slower at rest than an unhealthy organ, and for most of us there is only one way to achieve the former: regular exercise. This also reduces cholesterol and helps to flush fatty deposits out of the arteries. The Harvard Alumni Health Study, which has tracked the health of 17,000 men for twenty years, has found that each hour of exercise (up to thirty hours a week) extends life expectancy by approximately two hours.

Understandably, those who build up lavish deposits before they undertake to flush them out can be risking their lives. But the chance of keeling over and dying during the London or New York marathons is still only around one in 100,000.[42] This is rather better odds than the estimated one in

15,000 chance of dropping dead during ordinary jogging,[43] or the one in 18,000 chance of expiring during exercise in general.[44] Although any individual – seasoned runners included – is more likely to suffer a heart attack during a marathon than while sitting in front of the television, they are far less likely to suffer an attack over the course of their lifetime if they spend part of it running and training for marathons. Medical authorities acknowledge that mildly impaired heart function persists for up to one month after completing a race, but not to a degree thought dangerous for anyone free of coronary disease. One also finds tissue stress after performing dumb-bell curls, but no one thinks that such exercise is bad for the biceps. A study found that 81 per cent of those who suffered heart attacks during marathons had ignored warning symptoms such as chest pains and dizziness.[45] Jim Fixx himself had continued to train despite several smaller heart attacks.

Unfortunately, cardiac arrest is not the only danger a marathon runner faces. Dehydration was once thought to be the reason why some athletes collapse at the end of an endurance race. In fact, it is caused by blood accumulating in the lower legs and feet when the heart slows down as the runner draws to a halt. After an ultramarathon, medical teams are no longer advised to quickly administer intravenous fluids, but simply to make sure that they lay the athlete down with his feet higher than his head. Most people then soon perk up. The real problem with dehydration is that it frustrates the body's efforts to cool itself. In hot conditions, or when high humidity impedes the evaporation of sweat, the body might cook itself. A marathon runner can finish a race with a body temperature of 105°F (40°C). Another couple of degrees and he or she can faint or even die. It is easy enough to guard against overheating by drinking plenty of water throughout the race. But if you drink too much you might suffer hyponatraemia, or water intoxication, as the salt in your blood becomes too diluted – especially if you are a slowcoach and spend more time on the course, drinking as you go. This fate will befall around 0.3 per cent of runners, and with fields upwards of 30,000 in the London Marathon, this means that we can expect ninety cases of varying severity in a single event. The only competitor to die after the 2007 race was a 22-year-old fitness instructor who overhydrated. Hyponatraemia means that a competitor can actually put on weight during a race.

The risks for most marathon runners are more mundane. The body's efforts to repair muscle tissue damaged during a race suppresses the immune system for between three hours and three days.[46] Coupled with finding oneself in a throng of puffing bodies during a race, this trebles one's chance of catching a cold or a throat infection. This is hardly the stuff of medical emergency, but the cynic has a last resort that every runner can relate to: the human body was never designed to run on hard surfaces. Tarmac does not occur in nature. Our ancestors were used to feeling the earth of the savannah beneath their feet, not the joint-smashing roads and bone-shaking pavements of the modern marathon that exact a punishing toll on our shins, knees and vertebrae. Skeletal injuries are indeed common in marathon runners, but the evidence suggests that they usually do not cause permanent damage. The most common site of an injury is the knee, yet regular marathon running has been found to halve the long-term incidence of arthritis in the knees.[47]

One explanation is that humans evolved for distance

running. On the ancient savannah, hunting was less a matter of throwing spears at animals than wearing them down in gruelling pursuits lasting several hours. The palaeontologist Richard Leakey once demonstrated this when he ran down an antelope by keeping a slow but relentless pace. Leakey was the outdoors type, but most healthy individuals could replicate his feat. During the 2007 London Marathon, the notorious reality TV star Jade Goody jogged the first eight miles of the course before spending four hours walking the next ten. At this point, she collapsed in pain and reportedly screamed 'I'm dying! I'm dying!' as she was bundled into an ambulance and rushed to hospital. Her preparations for the race had involved Chinese takeaways, curries, lager and, in her own words, 'hardly any' training. It is easy to forget that she still managed to run eight miles. Admittedly, the human ability to outrun an antelope is partly down to our greater intelligence: the animal will tend to flee in a series of energy-sapping sprints rather than keeping a constant distance and pacing itself. One can easily imagine the hapless Jade attempting to catch the creature with a series of sprints of her own.

Which sport has the fittest participants?

The sport of triathlon began with an argument between a group of US Navy Seals in San Diego. They wondered who were the fittest – swimmers, runners or cyclists – and attempted to find a way to answer the question. The solution they thrashed out was to conduct races in all three disciplines and see which they found the hardest. Furthermore, they would compete in each event consecutively which, while hardly scientific, certainly appealed to their machismo – especially when their commander decided to award the title of 'Ironman' to the winner. The first formally organized ironman race to invite all comers was staged in 1978, when fifteen entrants paid $3 each to attempt a 2.4-mile swim, a 112-mile bike ride and a 26.2-mile run under the Hawaiian sun. All but three entrants made it to the finish.

Scientists would later settle the Navy Seals' debate from the comfort of their laboratory, but not before television had a go. The popular BBC television programme *Superstars* has been running for over three decades, pitting top sports personalities against one another in a selection of events. In the 2005 series, each competitor took part in six out of eight disciplines – sitting out the one most similar to their own sport and one further event of their choice. The events comprised kayaking, sprinting, swimming, gym tests and mountain biking, plus the shot put, football and cross-country running. In the final, the latter three were replaced by tennis, golf and basketball. Regrettably, no pattern has emerged since the hurdler David Hemery won the inaugural contest. Since then, the *Superstars* title has been held by a boxer, a rower, a judo expert, a pole-vaulter, a snowboarder, a skier, two swimmers, two rugby players and two 400-metre runners.

'Fitness' is a term that refers to five traits: cardiovascular efficiency, muscle to fat ratio, strength, agility and flexibility. In this sense, there are different kinds of fitness for different sports, yet researchers have tacitly agreed upon a common currency. The preferred unit of measurement when comparing different athletes' fitness is 'VO_2 max' – the maximum volume of oxygen that one can consume while exercising, expressed in terms of millilitres of oxygen per kilogram of bodyweight per minute. In 1996, a team at the University of Paris compared the VO_2 max of groups of national-class cyclists, runners, swimmers and kayakers.[48] There was little to separate the runners and cyclists, but the former had the edge over the latter with an average of 74.9 ml/kg compared to 72.4 ml/kg. Both were well ahead of the swimmers (59.6 ml/kg) and kayakers (53.8 ml/kg).

However, the researchers acknowledged that the cyclists were hamstrung by their larger body masses in this particular trial and the fact that they were operating in winter, out of season. Under different circumstances, they would normally beat the runners. For example, another study of top German cyclists gave an average VO_2 max of 78 ml/kg.[49] Lance Armstrong's VO_2 max is 83.8. He also boasts a resting heart rate of 32 beats per minutes – compared with 60–70 for the average man – which rises to 201 at full exertion. According to his biographer Dan Coyle, these attributes make him 'the world's greatest human power plant'. He needed to be to win the Tour de France a record seven consecutive times. As Coyle put it:

> The Tour is the hardest event on the planet, nothing comes close. Studies have shown that Tour riders spend more daily energy than Everest climbers. During those three weeks they spend energy at a rate that exceeds the capabilities of all but four animal species. Imagine running a marathon a day for 20 days. The food alone is ridiculous: on big days, they eat the equivalent of 28 cheeseburgers.[50]

As unlikely as it seems, there is indeed something harder, for cyclists are not quite the fittest athletes in terms of VO_2 max. That honour goes to cross-country skiers. Since they must use their arms as well as their legs to propel themselves, they are sending oxygen to the entire body. A study of elite German biathletes – a sport in which competitors also have to be skilled in rifle shooting and so can be expected to fall below the standards of pure skiers – found an average VO_2 max of 81.7 among a group of six men.[51] The fittest of them was on a par with Lance Armstrong. Pure cross-country skiers have reported scores of over 90 ml/kg.

Was soccer hooliganism ever the English disease?

When Lazio's Sinisa Mihajlovic racially abused Arsenal's Patrick Vieira during a Champions League match in 2000, what angered a section of the Italian fans more than anything was his subsequent public apology. At a late season home game against Bari, the referee called a halt to play when a racist banner was unfurled across half the length of a stand and angry scenes broke out between rival Lazio factions. Such scenes would now be unthinkable at an English football ground. But while other countries are now experiencing the hooligan problems that English clubs faced in the seventies and eighties, there seems to be little doubt over who first exported the phenomenon.

Whenever there is trouble involving English fans abroad, they are invariably painted as the perpetrators rather than the victims. Even when two innocent Leeds United supporters were stabbed to death by Turkish fans in Istanbul in 2000, local reaction was ambivalent to say the least, with the families of the accused reportedly blaming the visitors. The reputation that precedes English fans has reached such proportions that prior to the 2002 World Cup in Japan, 54,000 litres of glue was allocated to be poured onto the stones along 3.5 kilometres of railway tracks in Osaka to prevent them from being picked up and used as weapons by hooligans.

The signature event that created this reputation was the Heysel Stadium disaster of 1985. Before the European Cup Final kicked off, a group of Liverpool fans attacked the Juventus crowd and drove them into a wall which then collapsed, killing thirty-nine people and injuring hundreds. Lest the tragedy be put down to misadventure, television footage also showed Liverpool supporters beating Italian fans over the head with metal poles torn from the stadium. Had English clubs not been banned from European competition as a result, Prime Minister Margaret Thatcher was ready to force them to withdraw in their own right. At that moment in history, traditional English self-criticism coincided with continental Anglophobia.

A gleeful media reminded Britain that soccer had its roots in medieval mob football, the violent large-scale confrontations between hundreds of men from opposing villages. A French observer of a match in Derby in 1829 asked, 'If this is what they call football, what do they call fighting?'[52] There was a brief period of regulated gentility in the late nineteenth century when the public-school educated aristocracy dominated the game, but rowdiness soon reappeared. Crowd disturbances were a regular feature of the game even during the relatively sedate inter-war years, when the weapons of choice were half-pint stout bottles. Since then football violence has been pronounced dead on more than one occasion only to lurch back to life and throttle the coroner. On Saturday 5 May 1990, the *Independent* ran a story that 'hooliganism is not fashionable any more'. Presumably, the three thousand Leeds United fans who rioted in Bournemouth later that day did not read the *Independent*.

It has been a great disappointment to the media that, recently, fans have usually declined to go on the rampage in foreign cities. Police have learned to identify and isolate the worst offenders before they can get to foreign tournaments, but this has not stopped more English fans following their team abroad than those of any other nation. As many as 100,000 people travelled to Germany for the 2006 World Cup. In 2002, the Japanese police did not have to use their glue in anger. UEFA's Director of Communications praised the English fans' behaviour at Euro 2004 in Portugal and awarded them '9 out of 10 for behaviour'. This was no thanks to the best efforts of the nation's tabloid reporters. One photographer allegedly offered a fan £150 to kick a German, while another was paid to wrap himself in a flag of St George and lie on the pavement, pretending to be drunk.[53] Stories of police brutality against the English now outstrip the hooligans' own misdemeanours. The late Tory minister Alan Clark was being quite serious when he talked of the 'courage' of English football fans who fought off the Italian carabinieri after they were attacked without provocation during a World Cup qualifier in Rome in 1997.

Even considering the darkest days of the eighties, soccer-related violence in many other countries has matched or exceeded what has been seen in England. Of the major European nations, only Norway has avoided any large-scale disturbances, barring one occasion in 1993 when forty-one fans were arrested after a hot-dog stand was robbed. Scottish fans have been especially good at public relations. The 1977 pitch invasion at Wembley and the destruction of the goalposts is remembered with an affection that would never have featured had it been English supporters behaving in the same way at Hampden Park. Scotland's 'Tartan Army' is known for its good-natured mingling with foreign supporters, yet when the ginger wigs are removed the knives come out. Since 1996, there have been eight murders following Auld Firm derbies alone. One Glasgow Rangers fan convicted of slitting the throat of a 16-year-old Celtic supporter subsequently applied to be moved to an Ulster jail as a political prisoner. English skinheads were no slouches either when it came to bigotry on the terraces, but it is unlikely that their number ever matched the 20 per cent of German fans expressing sympathy with the neo-Nazi movement in one survey.[54] Neither has there been anything quite like the incident in Moscow following Russia's defeat by Japan at the 2002 World Cup. Gangs of thugs scoured the streets of the city for anyone of oriental appearance whom they could subject to a beating. They found fifty-two people, two of whom died from their injuries.

The Turkish supporters of Galatasaray are famed for their banners greeting visiting teams with the words 'Welcome to Hell', a threat they made good on when several fans managed to assault Manchester United's Eric Cantona and Bryan Robson in the players' tunnel during a tie in 1993. But the country's worst outbreak of football violence occurred in the fifties. Rival supporters from the Kayseri and Sivas clubs fought running battles with knives, broken bottles and pistols that lasted several days and brought streets to ruin. By the time the army was called in to restore order, forty-two fans were dead and six hundred injured. It is no wonder that in the sixties it was English clubs that considered pulling out of European competition for fear of violence by foreign supporters.

This is the worst Europe has to offer, but it is a mere skirmish compared with some of the violence witnessed in Africa and South America. After a Peruvian goal was disallowed two minutes from time during a match against Argentina in 1964, the home supporters started a riot in which 318 people were killed. The terraces of Brazil too have been subject to sporadic shootings and even kidnappings over the years, and the deciding game of the 2000 championship was abandoned due to crowd violence. The Rio state governor resisted police requests to send in the army on that occasion, but there is now a special mobile court system in the state of Pernambuco to try soccer hooligans on the spot. In 2000, the final of the African women's championship had to be abandoned after South African fans rioted. One year later, over 150 people were killed during a pitched battle between supporters of Ghanaian rivals Hearts of Oak and Asante Kotoko. A blackout in Nigeria during an international friendly led to civil unrest and barricades in the streets in the south of the country in 2002. When power cuts threatened coverage of the 2002 World Cup, the national electricity supplier took out full-page ads in the national press urging fans: 'Please don't take the law into your own hands. If you go on an orgy of destruction simply because there was a power failure during a favourite match you may be watching, you will not be helping matters.' The difference in Africa is that most incidents seem to be spontaneous and sparked by refereeing decisions rather than the organizing efforts of hooligan leaders.

Outside England, the most organized trouble has involved Italian and Argentinian hooligan firms. Only in Argentina are hooligan groups, or *barras bravas*, part of the official administration of club teams. Argentinian clubs are ruled by their membership, and the most vocal and aggressive members are often the thug element. The Boca Juniors 'supporters' club, La Doce ('Player Number 12'), boasts more than two thousand members and was once so powerful that it forced the club to make Diego Maradona captain. Maradona remains close friends with La Doce's leaders. The stranglehold of the *barras bravas* saw fifty people murdered at football matches in the country in the nineties alone. In Italy, Internazionale's Ultras once threw a petrol bomb at their own team's coach after a 6-1 defeat to Parma in the Italian Cup. In 2001, they hurled a moped from the top tier of the San Siro stadium, narrowly missing supporters below. Two hundred and two Italian police officers were injured at matches in 2006, and matters came to a head when one was murdered during a riot in Catania, Sicily the following year. That death – one of eleven in domestic Italian competitions since the seventies – prompted a suspension of the entire national league.

For all this litany of shame, other than the rivalry between German and Dutch fans, most soccer-related violence around the world has been kept in the family and reserved for domestic fixtures. Ultras make an exception only when the English come to town. Thus most international football violence has involved the English, whether as instigators or victims. This is fitting given the role of English hooligans in the history of the subculture. For where crowd trouble has been commonplace around the world, it rarely had the deliberate focus brought by Chelsea's Headhunters or West Ham's Inter City Firm. In the seventies and eighties, the ever-present risks associated with large groups of young men in various states of drunkenness took on a different character. Where violence had been a result of the groups, the groups were now a result of the violence. And the ethos spread to the rest of Europe as copycat gangs relabelled their thuggish instincts. For example, Dutch hooliganism was in part seeded by the behaviour of the Tottenham Hotspur fans who rioted in Rotterdam in 1974.

Tragically, Heysel seems to have acted as a catalyst for the formation of hooligan groups across the continent and for the escalation of those that already existed. The Social Issues Research Centre notes that in Portugal, a nation that was free from soccer violence until relatively recently, hooligan graffiti is often written in English – a language that few fans can actually speak or understand. As a report by Belgium's Leuven University in 1983 put it, 'all the lines lead back to British hooligans. They are seen as the professionals. They are the great example to hooligans from all over the rest of Europe.'[55] It seems that soccer hooliganism was called the 'English Disease' because only the English strain was communicable.

Why do they geld racehorses?

When the great Red Rum was retired from racing, his many fans said that they would never see another horse like him. They were quite right. The nation's favourite Grand National winner would never sire an heir to the Aintree course because, like most of his National Hunt compatriots, he was a gelding. Red Rum died in 1995, but had he lived through the announcement of the world's first cloned horse in Italy in May 2003 this would not have changed matters. Artificial breeding methods are banned in thoroughbred racing, which also means that there would have been no point in freezing his sperm prior to castration. The decision to geld, then, is final. Yet top thoroughbreds can make far more in their retirement at stud farms than in prize money from their races, so owners obviously need a very good reason before they ensure that their property will never reproduce.

Some colts suffer from undescended testicles that cause discomfort and make castration necessary, but medical reasons are not chief among the reasons for gelding. Although occasionally a horse will go to stud without ever having raced, most thoroughbreds first need to prove themselves on the track. But stallions can sometimes be so highly strung that they are in no shape for racing, preferring to concentrate on fighting other males and mating with the mares. Gelding such animals at least gives the owner a chance to recoup some of his investment through prize money. Stallions are also more difficult to train and look after and can cause problems when stabled next to other horses – so much so that some trainers recommend that all stallions are gelded unless they are going to be handled solely by professionals.

Geldings develop less muscle than stallions, but this does not impair their athleticism since they develop less impeding bulk around their forequarters, which is helpful in jumping and in endurance events. They are forbidden from competing in the five 'Classic' flat races in Britain and the Prix de l'Arc de Triomphe, but this is less due to their inferiority on the track than the stud potential for winners that would be wasted on geldings. However, many National Hunt racehorses are indeed rejects from the far more lucrative flat. The need to castrate jumpers such as Red Rum and Desert Orchid, as well as those used in equestrianism, is more obvious, since it is paramount that they be controllable. Also, a stallion could suffer a painful injury when his hindquarters clear a hedge.

Desert Orchid and Red Rum would never have had such long racing careers had they been stallions packed off to stud, and would not have had time to win the public's affection. Whether the affection of racegoers is an adequate substitute for that of mares is another question.

Should performance-enhancing drugs be allowed in sport?

Performance-enhancing substances have been a feature of sport ever since the Ancient Greeks forced down plates of sheep's testicles to give themselves an edge in the Olympic Games. Today's competitors are prepared to go even further. In a 1996 survey of 198 Olympic athletes past and present, 98 per cent said that they would take a new drug that would guarantee victory even if it would lead to their death within five years.[56] The difference is that sheep genitalia were part of a legal training regime, whereas in the modern era performance-enhancing drugs have been prohibited since the International Amateur Athletic Federation outlawed 'stimulating substances' in 1928. This has partly been out of a concern for athletes' health. In the 1904 Games, the USA's Thomas Hicks won the marathon but nearly died from the brandy and strychnine he had consumed en route to the finishing line. Tom Simpson fell dead from his saddle in the 1967 Tour de France after fortifying himself with brandy and amphetamines. But the rationale stems chiefly from the Olympic movement's amateur roots and the notion of fair play. It is this that makes the current zero tolerance approach to doping arbitrary, ill-considered and ultimately doomed.

It has also been called 'unfounded, dangerous, and excessively costly'. These words came not from Ben Johnson's lawyers, but from a group of medical experts writing in *The Lancet*.[57] Athletes should not be forced to risk their health in order to compete at the highest level. However, there is widespread suspicion that they are already required to do this due to the inability of the authorities to catch all but a handful of the perpetrators. The consensus among athletes is that cheating is rife in their sport. They suspect that many of the guilty go undetected due to increasingly sophisticated doping methods, while others suffer a false positive or break the rules inadvertently. The Scottish skier Alain Baxter even lost his Olympic bronze medal in 2002 because he had used an American Vicks inhaler that contained a banned substance not featured in the British version. According to the lawyer who defended the Greek sprinter Kostas Kenteris against the charge of dodging a dope test, 'the athlete who wins is the athlete who has the best chemist and the best lawyer'.[58]

The *Lancet* group claims there is a solution: 'We believe,' they continued, 'that rather than drive doping underground, use of drugs should be permitted under medical supervision.' This is not to say that no risks are involved, but 'sport is dangerous even if no drugs are taken – playing soccer comes with high risks for knee and ankle problems, for instance, and boxing can lead to brain damage.' Soon afterwards Julian Savulescu, Oxford University's Professor of Practical Ethics, told the *Financial Times*: 'I would prefer my child to take anabolic steroids and growth hormone than play rugby. Growth hormone is safer than rugby. At least I don't know of any cases of quadriplegia caused by growth hormone.'[59] Some drugs are actually permitted despite known dangers. For example, athletes are allowed to receive painkilling injections into their joints that could increase the long-term risk of arthritis. The decision to accept one form of risk but not another is at best arbitrary, and given that little can be done to stop either type of risk-taking, a policy that prevents the implementation of safeguards in one case is irresponsible.

It is also arbitrary to allow one form of 'unfair' advantage but not another. Not every athlete has access to the latest equipment or the most effective training methods, yet the IOC does not talk of banning, say, altitude chambers for distance runners. In some events, the gains bestowed by advanced sports equipment such as hi-tech bicycles and sharkskin-effect swimming suits can outweigh even those achievable with performance-enhancing drugs. In 1972, the Belgian cyclist Eddy Merckx set a world record for distance cycled in one hour, covering 49.431 km. This mark was subsequently broken and rebroken by cyclists using more technologically advanced bikes. But in 2000, cycling's authorities decided to reinstate Merckx's record and recognize only improvements made with comparable equipment. The record is currently held by Britain's Chris Boardman, who that year managed to beat it by the wafer-thin margin of ten metres. However, Boardman smashed the record by almost seven kilometres in a variant of the event when he was allowed to use the latest technology, including a special aerodynamic helmet. On this evidence alone, technology has been responsible for a 14 per cent improvement in performance over the last twenty-five years.

Bespoke superbikes, altitude chambers and foreign training camps are all far more expensive than courses of performance-enhancing drugs. Such equipment is often out of reach for athletes from developing countries, while richer nations can spend their way to success. For example, in the four years before the 2004 Athens Olympics, Australia spent AU$547 million on sports funding. The result was seventeen gold medals effectively achieved at AU$32 million a piece. This placed the country in fourth place in the medals table despite its small population (fifty-second largest in the world).

The unfairness of the current system is not just economic, for athletic gifts are not distributed equally among the world's population. The highest levels of sporting competition are something of a freak show. For example, the swimmer Ian Thorpe's size 17 feet propel him through the water faster than a more daintily hoofed rival can manage, yet because he does not use drugs he 'deserves' to win. Cricket's best bowler of all time, Muttiah Muralitharan, has achieved a Test bowling average of 21.73 with the help of a congenitally deformed elbow that gives him a unique action. It also prevents him from straightening his arm fully, but rather than declare his action illegal, cricket's authorities changed the rules to allow bowlers a 15-degree bend in their arm when the ball is released. In the sixties, Finland's Eero Mäntyranta won three Olympic gold medals in cross-country skiing. Possessing phenomenal endurance and known for his relentless training methods, Mäntyranta was long suspected of 'blood doping' – the practice of transfusing extra red blood cells to increase oxygen uptake and stamina. In one test, his blood contained 15 per cent more red cells than other athletes', but there was no other evidence of cheating. In 1993, researchers ran a DNA test on 200 members of the skier's family and concluded that he possessed a genetic mutation that gave him up to 50 per cent more red blood cells than the average man. This quirk of nature gave Mäntyranta an advantage that would have been insurmountable to anyone who did not employ illegal doping methods. This is why Oxford's Professor Savulescu and his colleagues argue that a controlled legalization of certain drugs would 'level the playing field'.[60]

There are several ways to boost one's red blood cell count. Training at altitude or using a hypoxic air machine to simulate those conditions makes a significant difference, as does having a transfusion of one's own blood collected a few weeks earlier. Such 'autologous' doping cannot be detected. Or one could use illegal injections of erythropoietin (EPO), a hormone that stimulates the bone marrow to produce more red cells. The point is that there is no essential difference between any of these methods. The blood cells acquired will be the same whatever prompted their production. EPO is already made by the kidneys and occurs naturally in the body. Here, as with many of the latest drugs, there is no defensible distinction between natural and unnatural substances. Some athletes are lucky enough to boast an innate abundance of certain hormones. They are effectively born with drugs coursing through their veins. Their good fortune does not make them more virtuous and morally deserving of victory than those who require extra help. A more virtuous attitude to doping regulation, however, would set a maximum level of red blood cells for fair competition rather than policing where they came from. If anything, Ben Johnson deserved to win more than Carl Lewis in 1984 because he trained harder than the man he 'cheated'.

A former British sprinter once asked the *Observer* newspaper's correspondent, 'Do spectators and TV viewers want to see normal people running? Do they really want to see the Olympic 100 metres gold won in 10.2 seconds? No. They want to see monsters fuelled by steroids making super-human performances and winning races in 9.75. That's the reality.'[61] One hopes that it is not and that most sports fans want to watch recognizably human competitors to whom they can relate. But we should not fool ourselves that the current arrangements are right and just.

Why is a duck the most common cricket score?

The former West Indies fast bowler Courtney Walsh held the record for the most Test wickets taken until 2004, when his total was surpassed by Sri Lanka's Muttiah Muralitharan. However, Walsh retains another world record that he would be only too willing to part with: no one else has scored more ducks in Test cricket. He recorded 43 in all, but with an average of just 7.53 runs he was never noted for his prowess with the bat. We should not be surprised that a duck is the most common score for a bowler, but there is a debate among some fans and commentators over why the story is the same for the world's top batsmen. Almost every cricketer scores more of them than any other total, with England's Alistair Cook being an extremely rare exception. As of 17 May 2007, Cook is yet to score zero in twenty-eight innings in Test cricket, but his Test career is still young.

A layperson might expect a cricketer's modal score – their most common total – to more or less match their mean (their average tally of runs), but the two rarely get close. In 232 Test innings between December 1990 and November 2006, Brian Lara's batting average was 52.89. He scored 52 only three times and 53 just twice, but he was out for a duck seventeen times. Sachin Tendulkar scored thirteen ducks in 219 innings on the way to acquiring an average of 54.82. He has scored 54 and 55 twice apiece. Ricky Ponting has eight ducks from 183 innings, but he has scored 59 once and 60 only twice on his way to an average of 59.29. Of the world's best batsmen, only India's Rahul Dravid bucks the trend with eight scores of 2. But zero is still his second most common score. Even the greatest batsman of all time, Don Bradman, scored seven ducks in eighty Test innings, including his final effort at the crease that left him a sliver away from a Test average of 100. Bradman never finished dead on a century, or on 99 or 101 for that matter.

There are a number of bogus explanations for the prevalence of ducks. Some commentators believe that a batsman's first few minutes at the crease are especially perilous because he has yet to 'get his eye in' and bowlers might make a special effort to get a new player out before he can settle. But the answer to the curse of the duck lies in simple mathematics. A cricketer faces at least one ball on zero every time he bats, and he must face it before he can get the chance to play off a different score. Some scores will be skipped if he makes boundaries. Naturally, more deliveries will be faced on zero than on any other total, and this means that there is a greater chance of getting out on a duck than of making any other score.

Do some darts players actually need to drink alcohol?

When Britain's first academy of excellence for young darts players opened in 2006, the organizer John Gibbs assured journalists that the only drinks available would be non-alcoholic. Gibbs admitted to drinking twenty-two pints of beer in a session in his youth, but explained: 'The days are gone when darts players had a fag in their mouth, a pint of beer in their hand and a big belly.' They hadn't been gone for very long, however, as it was only two years before that the British Darts Organisation (BDO) World Championship had been won by 30-stone Andy 'the Viking' Fordham, whose preparations for a match involved downing twenty-five bottles of export-strength lager. Before he took up darts, Fordham was reportedly a promising young track and field athlete nicknamed 'the whippet'. But at the peak of his powers as a world-class sportsman he suffered from acute chest pains and breathing difficulties and pulled out of the 2005 World Championship after fainting from heat exhaustion.

In Martin Amis's novel *London Fields*, the darts-obsessed Keith Talent drinks 'to loosen the throwing arm'. He explains that this makes it 'part of his job'. From watching the sport on television over the years, it is easy to understand his misconception. As Eric Bristow once said, 'You can take darts out of the pub, but you can't take the pub out of darts.' Two-time world champion Jocky Wilson seemed to drink non-stop during his matches, usually pints of lager with vodka and Coke chasers, all to 'steady the nerves'. He also tried to smoke his way through as many cigarettes as possible out of the 200 a day he was given by his sponsors, Embassy. Toothless from the age of 28, Wilson preferred to leave his dentures out because they made him belch when he drank.

When Phil 'the Power' Taylor, the game's greatest ever player, lost the 2003 Professional Darts Corporation (PDC) World Final to John Part, the commentator Sid Waddell blamed it on the champion's weight-loss regime that had seen him shed three stone in four months: 'He's lost muscle weight below the navel and that has affected his balance. He now often throws a quarter to half an inch below the 60 bed.'[62] But Taylor himself blamed his defeat on a tough year emotionally and now swears by regular visits to the gym.

Taking good care of oneself is now reasonably normal practice among the younger players on the circuit. The authorities behind darts are so pleased with the change in the game's image that they are pressing for it to be included in the London Olympics in 2012. 'I might smoke and I might drink,' said Martin Adams, captain of the England darts team, 'but what has that got to do with anything? Not all darts players are fat and lazy. The young ones are a new generation that does not drink before a match. They are extremely fit and competitive.'[63] In January 2006, even Andy Fordham told a reporter: 'I am determined to keep off the weight until we make it to the Olympics. It's a new lifestyle. I can't completely cut out the booze because I get nervous before a match and need a drink to calm the nerves. I know we would trash any other country at darts if we got into the Olympics. Darts is not just about throwing arrows and hoping for the best. It's a highly skilled game that we have to play under intense heat of lights; you need serious stamina.'[64]

The biggest drinkers in darts have tended to be very large men who can handle the alcohol reasonably well. They can play to a high standard despite, rather than due to, the amount they take in. Cliff Lazarenko is a case in point. The commentator Sid Waddell named Lazarenko as the thirstiest man in the game; he would routinely prepare with either twenty cans of lager or six to eight pints of Strongbow, finishing off the tenth pint by the end of a match (downing the extras during the commercial breaks after drinking on screen was banned). Yet Waddell claimed that he had never once seen Lazarenko drunk. The late snooker player Bill Werbeniuk, a 20-stone chain-smoker, was famous for imbibing prodigious amounts before and during matches. He claimed that he needed the alcohol to suppress a tremor in his arm, and even tried to claim his drink expenses against tax. After his last professional game in 1990, he said, 'I've had twenty-four pints of extra-strong lager and eight double vodkas and I'm still not drunk.'

Oddly, competitors in most other sports that require superlative hand–eye coordination, such as Olympic pistol and rifle shooting, have never claimed that they need to polish off bottles of vodka to 'steady their hands'. Andy Fordham's successor in the 2006 BDO World Championships was Jelle Klaasen – a teetotal, non-smoking, 10-stone Dutchman. Clearly, drinking heavily is not essential for success at the highest level.

Why are there two rugby codes?

Rugby's split into two codes, league and union, followed a meeting of delegates from the leading northern English clubs in 1895 at the George Hotel in Huddersfield. A crisis had arisen over the issue of professionalism. The northern clubs had demanded to be allowed to compensate their working-class players for loss of earnings during the time they spent playing, training and, more importantly, recovering from injuries. But the game's upper- and middle-class authorities, based in the south, resolutely refused to compromise their amateur status. Rather than suffer a disadvantage, and in protest at the unfairness, twenty-two clubs broke away to form the Northern Union, which soon became fully professional (as, confusingly, the Rugby League).

Arguments over which code is superior have continued ever since. Union has enjoyed most of the glamour, international recognition and, since 1996 when it too turned professional, money. Where union talents once left for a payday in the league, the traffic is now almost all one-way in the other direction. Outside Great Britain, league is played professionally only in Australia, Ireland, France and New Zealand, though it is also the national game of Papua New Guinea. However, league has always had an image problem, a victim of snobbish attitudes. Union fans should note that the reason league has different rules is because they were introduced to make the game more entertaining for the paying spectators. League matches involve more attacking and running with the ball – the very elements that union supporters (especially England fans) say they'd like more of. It is also more physically demanding. According to former Wales centre Jason Critchley, a player of both codes, 'The union boys are just as hard, but league can be a lot tougher on the body.'[65] He has a list of injuries from league to prove it – including restructured cheekbones and a metal plate in his left hand.

In May 1996, Wigan and Bath held two exhibition matches, with a different code used in each. In the match at Maine Road under league rules, Wigan slaughtered Bath 82-6 and then lost 44-19 at Twickenham in the union leg. The fitness of the Wigan players was generally agreed to be superior to that of their union counterparts. However, now union is fully professional there is no such disparity. Former Wigan and Great Britain league captain Andrew Farrell said, 'I used to think it was boring. And there's that north–south thing, which is stupid, really. But I learnt a lot in that game against Bath about how technical it is – the rucking, the mauling, the line-outs, the scrummaging. It's a completely different game, in fact. You score tries, kick goals, play with an oval ball, and that's about it. Not half of those playing rugby union could play rugby league, and not three-quarters of those playing rugby league could play rugby union.'[66] This has not stopped many from trying in recent years – including Farrell himself. Farrell moved to the union side Saracens in 2005, but his subsequent performances for England fell short of what might have been expected from the most 'complete' of league players. He is yet to find a position in which he is comfortable, having failed to develop the technical skills required of a flanker and lacking the speed to play in the back line. As a centre he was made to look slow in his country's 43-13 defeat by Ireland in Dublin in February 2007.

Other high-profile code changes such as those of Henry Paul and Wales's Iestyn Harris have been similarly uninspiring. It would seem to be no bad thing that talk of a merger between the two codes has evaporated.

Can transsexuals compete as women in the Olympics?

When the US runner Helen Stephens broke the 100 metres world record to win gold in the 1936 Olympics in Berlin, her beaten rival and previous record holder, Poland's Stanislawa Walasiewicz, accused her of being a man in disguise. Walasiewicz's words were taken seriously and Nazi officials were forced to perform a sex check on the new champion. This seems to have involved Adolf Hitler himself, who invited Stephens to his private box. Although she met his Nazi salute with a handshake, he reportedly gave her a 'squeeze, pinch, hug and full massage'. He declared that she was a 'true Aryan type and should be running for Germany', after which she had to politely decline his invitation to spend the weekend with him in the Eagle's Nest at Berchtesgaden.[67] The Führer does not seem to have been a stickler for gender in any case. It was at the same Olympics that the Hitler Youth induced Hermann Ratjen to bind his genitals and enter the women's high jump event as 'Dora'. He finished fourth. Ironically, after Stephens' accuser, then living as Stella Walsh in the US, was shot dead in 1980 as she witnessed a robbery, an autopsy revealed that she herself was a man.

Sex-testing began in 1966 when the International Amateur Athletics Federation decided to act on increasing public speculation that cheating was rife among Soviet teams. Before the European Track and Field Championships, every female competitor was required to parade naked before a panel of female doctors. The public's suspicions were confirmed when six Eastern Bloc athletes immediately withdrew from the competition and announced their retirement rather than submit to the test. These included the hulking Press 'sisters' – Tamara, the gold medal winning shot-putter and discus thrower, and Irina, the 100 metres hurdles champion. But some of the legendary 'stubbly' East German shot-putters did not start out as men. Heidi Krieger – the winner of the 1986 European Championship – had been made to take so many steroids and male hormones by her trainers that she developed facial hair and an Adam's apple. She eventually decided to have a sex change operation and renamed herself 'Andreas'.

The IOC introduced laboratory tests on cell samples for the Mexico Olympics in 1968, and after these proved inconclusive they were replaced by chromosomal analysis. One of the earliest to suffer was the chromosomally male Austrian Erika Schinegger, who was banned from the Olympics two years after winning the 1966 Women's Downhill Skiing World Championship. Princess Anne was the only female competitor in the 1976 Montreal Games not to have to undergo a sex test. However, even genetic testing produced ambiguous results. The Polish sprinter Eva Klobukowska passed a gynaecological examination in 1966 but was banned from athletic competition the following year for possessing a Y chromosome. The efficacy of chromosomal analysis was cast into doubt when she later gave birth.

One in 60,000 males is subject to 'androgen insensitivity', an immunity to testosterone that means they grow up to resemble females despite possessing a Y chromosome.[68] It is thought that androgen insensitivity denies the usual physical advantages that males possess over females, and seven such individuals were allowed to compete as women in the Atlanta Olympics in 1996. If this is thought unfair, then it is less so than allowing women with masculinizing genetic conditions to compete against their sisters. There is no doubt that, for example, adrenal hyperplasia confers an advantage over more feminine rivals, yet no one suggests banning athletes with the condition. Unable to devise a definitive sex test, the IOC finally abolished testing at the 2000 Olympics in Sydney.

In May 2004, the International Olympic Committee announced that, for the first time, transsexuals would be allowed to compete in all events in their reassigned gender. This was dependent upon them having completed genital reconstruction surgery and two years of hormone therapy. Their new gender also had to be legally recognized in their home country. The stipulation that surgery must have taken place was informed by a concern that if male-to-female transsexuals retained their testes, then they would have an advantage in testosterone production over their naturally female opponents. Similar levels of testosterone achieved through artificial means would swiftly see a female athlete banned for life for doping offences. But testosterone is not the only concern. Athletes who grew up as men have the male benefits of a larger frame, denser bones and a greater heart and lung capacity. These advantages are not completely wiped out by the hormone therapies that reduce muscle mass in male-to-female transsexuals. Which is why the former Olympic pentathlete Pat Connolly complains that 'It's the biggest insult to women and everything we've gone through. Gradually over the years, [the Olympics] started adding events for women. Why? To give women an opportunity to compete... Because there's an essential difference between men and women. Any dummy on the street knows the difference.'[69]

If there is really no advantage for a male-to-female transsexual in women's events, then we should ask why there have never been any women masquerading as men in Olympic competition. This is thought so unlikely that a contradiction has been left in the IOC's rules: transsexuals are allowed to compete provided they have been receiving hormone therapy for two years and yet the testosterone given to female-to-male transsexuals is regarded as a form of illegal doping. This testosterone does indeed cause performance-enhancing physiological changes such as increased thigh muscle mass and reduced body fat, but it is still not thought enough to enable individuals born as women to compete with those born as men. As yet there has been no flood of transsexuals in women's events. Not a single transgender athlete was reported to have competed in the Athens Games.

Are English footballers really thicker than foreign players?

'Football's like a big marketplace,' said Sir Bobby Robson, 'and people go to the market every day to buy their vegetables.' It isn't quite what he meant, but who could disagree given the exercise in inanity that is almost every post-match interview, where each player speaks in the same stock phrases and wears the same blank expression. A footballer diverts from this script at his own risk, as Graeme Le Saux discovered when he was branded a homosexual for reading a broadsheet newspaper and collecting antiques. David Beckham once admitted that he was stumped by his 6-year-old son's maths homework. This was the son of whom he said, 'I definitely want Brooklyn to be christened, but I don't know into what religion yet.' Despite expert help arranged by Real Madrid, Beckham still speaks only rudimentary Spanish. Language seems to be the key, because the low wattage of our stars really began to hit home with the influx of foreign players into the Premiership. For example, it was generally agreed that Jurgen Klinsmann spoke better English than his Tottenham Hotspur teammates.

By the 1998 World Cup, the view that the England team consistently underachieved because English players were too dim-witted to understand modern tactics had become commonplace. Stupidity was certainly the reason Beckham and

Wayne Rooney were sent off in 1998 and 2006 respectively, presaging England's exit from the tournament on both occasions. Strictly speaking, this had nothing to do with their intellectual grasp of formations and passing movements, but kicking or stamping on opponents in full view of the referee are perhaps exceptions that prove the rule.

Academic qualifications rarely feature on a professional footballer's CV, though you can find the odd boffin. Among recent players and managers, Iain Dowie has a master's degree in mechanical engineering, Steve Coppell took a degree in economics at Liverpool University while playing for Manchester United in the seventies, and Le Saux himself earned a degree in economics from Kingston University. Several players with less in the way of formal education such as Teddy Sheringham, Gareth Southgate and David James are all undeniably intelligent individuals. Robbie Fowler had the sense to invest his wages in building a property empire that at one time made him the richest person under thirty in the country according to the *Sunday Times* Rich List. Frank Lampard went to public school, where he achieved an A* in his Latin GCSE, though he was utterly baffled when asked on a quiz show, 'A bird in the hand is worth two in the what?'

At the other, thicker end of the wedge, so to speak, Jermaine Pennant was forced to reveal that he had never learned to read or write when he was convicted of drink-driving in 2005. At the time he was 22 years old and earning £10,000 a week at Arsenal. Schooling probably does not feel so important when you make your professional debut for Notts County at the age of 15 and are bought by a Premiership club for £2 million a year later. Success in soccer requires sacrifices at an early age, which is why so few middle-class youngsters go into the sport in the first place. Gianluca Vialli conducted a search for middle-class footballers in Britain and could find only the heir to the Walkers shortbread fortune, Nicky Walker, the Hearts goalkeeper during the nineties.[70] Middle-class youngsters are more likely to spend valuable soccer time being forced to do their homework or learn a musical instrument. They are also more likely to go to schools that play rugby rather than football. In the end, they have too much to lose to devote their lives to a sporting dream, at least as far as their parents are concerned, especially in an era when the first teams of the best clubs are filled with foreign imports. It is the latter more than anything else that has prompted the FA to improve young players' education in recent years. Since the majority of teenagers in football academies will fail to make the grade in today's top divisions, they need something to fall back on. In the future we can expect to see more players like Fulham's Liam Rosenior, who left school at 16 with nine GCSEs – five grade As and four A*s.

It's also worth asking whether the mental acuity of foreign players has been exaggerated. The Cameroon-born French international defender Jean-Alain Boumsong, formerly of Newcastle United, has a degree in mathematics, which he regards as his main interest outside football along with the works of Beethoven. But Boumsong is far from the norm. Arsenal's Swiss defender Philippe Senderos speaks five languages: English, Spanish, German, French and Italian. But the Swiss get German, French and Italian for 'free' as it were, and his father is Spanish. As for his rumoured philosophical interests, these consist not of the works of Wittgenstein or Nietzsche but the New Age claptrap of Paul Coelho – a firm believer in divine providence, possession by angels, and wild dogs that embody Satan.

The English are a modest race, and they tend to overrate language skills due to their own lack of them. Being bilingual does not by itself indicate a sharp mind, even though it is an unusual skill in this country. Nonetheless, Gary Lineker had no trouble learning Spanish at Barcelona. Neither did Steve McManaman at Real Madrid, and Paul Gascoigne made a better stab at Italian while at Lazio than most people suspect. Spain's biggest TV star is the Leicester-born sports pundit Michael Robinson, who played for Brighton, Liverpool and QPR in the eighties.

Simply being French is usually enough to win one a reputation for having a cultured mind. Thierry Henry is certainly a bright individual, but he was not academically gifted at school, where his results were so poor that the authorities had to make a special provision to allow him to attend the national football academy. Arsene Wenger himself is often mistaken for an intellectual when in fact he has few interests outside football. And few Gallic imports are as bright as Henry or Wenger. Eric Cantona's gnomic comments about seagulls and trawlers were greeted with a reverence they would not have enjoyed in his homeland where, to the native ear, his accent sounds more peasant than *pensant*.

As one manager put it, 'In every squad there are five completely stupid players, and at least one of those would end up begging on the streets if he didn't play professional football. From a twenty-five-man squad, two would be able to complete a university degree, and five to six would finish college. Around twelve would make a good living doing skilled manual labour or working as a bank clerk, but certainly five are completely stupid. This is the same for every team.' The manager in question was not Harry Redknapp or Sam Allardyce, but Hans Meyer of Hertha Berlin.[71]

Who would win in a fight between Muhammad Ali and Bruce Lee?

W hile preparing for his title defence against Joe Bugner in Malaysia in 1975, Muhammad Ali announced, 'I will prove to the world that I am not only the greatest boxer of all times, I am the greatest martial artist.' Then, before treating the kickboxer Davis Miller to a round of sparring, he declared, 'You must be a fool to get in the ring with me. When I'm through, you gowna think you been whupped by Bruce Lee.'[72] Miller reported how 'I bent to the right, tossed a jab toward his belt line, straightened, snapped a long, tentative front-kick to his head. I figured it was the first kick he'd ever had thrown at him, but he pulled away as easily as if he'd been dodging feet his entire life.' In that brief encounter, Ali allowed Miller to get a few hits in before knocking him senseless with two punches.

Bruce Lee would no doubt fare better than the young Miller did against the Greatest, but the end result would probably be no different. Ali stood 6'3" and weighed 236 pounds in his prime. Lee was 5'7" and just 135 pounds when he died. If Lee were a boxer he would be a lightweight – nine divisions below Ali's heavyweight class. In regular boxing there is a limited degree of movement between the weight divisions. Sugar Ray Leonard won world titles at five weights – welterweight, light middle, middle, super middle and light heavyweight – but he had to put on weight himself in order to be allowed to fight heavier opponents. There is also only 22 pounds between the closest limits of those categories – rather less than the 101 pounds Lee would be giving away to Ali. In 1920, the legendary Welsh flyweight Jimmy Wilde, 'the Mighty Atom', fought former world bantamweight champion Pete Herman in London. After being knocked out in the seventeenth round, Wilde modestly insisted that he had been beaten by the better boxer. However, he was more than a stone lighter than his opponent. The difference in weight was too much even for a fighter who went undefeated for 103 bouts and who regularly features in experts' all-time top ten lists. Boxing skills will rarely be enough to overcome a weight differential so long as both protagonists are ranking fighters. So the question is whether martial arts represents a superior form of skill to old-fashioned pugilism and whether any edge would be enough.

The first advantage people think of is the martial artist's ability to use kicks as well as punches. In any contest of champions, Muhammad Ali would be allowed to kick too – just as Bruce Lee would be allowed to punch – but one presumes he would rely on his fists. The second advantage is Lee's dazzling speed – though frames were cut from his fight scenes to make him appear even faster. Even so, his kicks could never be as fast as Ali's punches. This is no slight against the martial artist, but simply a reflection of human physiology and the laws of physics. Even the fastest kicks are slow compared to punches, because they require more build-up and begin from a greater distance from their target. Punches can also be followed up with more of the same, whereas combination kicks are slower, more difficult to execute and usually lose power.

Furthermore, Ali would be used to dodging punches that were much faster than Lee's kicks. So to bring his kicks to bear, Lee would need to keep Ali at a distance. Assuming that the two are fighting in a ring of limited size, Lee would probably not be able to keep out of the boxer's way for long enough. Ali himself was extremely fast for a heavyweight, but even he couldn't avoid dozens of punches from the lumbering George Foreman (realizing this, he even made it part of his game plan not to try to during their 'Rumble in the Jungle'). Similarly, no matter how fast Lee might be, he could not realistically be expected to dodge every blow from Ali. However, there is a tactic that he might have tried – one that was once actually employed against Ali in real life.

In 1975, two years after Lee's *Enter the Dragon* caused a sensation, Ali remarked that he would accept a challenge from 'any' oriental fighter. He was taken up on the offer by the Japanese wrestler Antonio Inoki and duly kept his word in an exhibition match over fifteen rounds in Tokyo. Ali's side were glad to take a reported $6 million as an inducement, but after witnessing Inoki's skills during a training session, they realized they were in trouble. At 224 pounds and 6'2" tall, Inoki was Ali's size, but what threatened to tip the balance was the man's ability to apply a chokehold and twist an arm out of its socket. Ali's handlers wisely insisted on a rule that the wrestler was not allowed to grapple. The result was a farce. Inoki spent most of the fight lying on his back in the middle of the ring, sending kicks into Ali's shins whenever the boxer approached, while Ali himself barely landed a punch. The contest was declared a draw, which represented a moral victory for Inoki as he had three points deducted for not moving. Widely believed to be a charade at the time, especially in Japan, the fight did lead to Ali having hospital treatment for blood clots in his legs.[73] Eleven years later, Inoki was set up with another heavyweight champion, Leon Spinks, and pinned him in the eighth round.

Had Inoki been allowed to use his normal wrestling moves against Ali, the outcome might have been very different. Instead of speaking about how many kicks Ali could withstand in order to get close to a martial artist and throw his punches, we would be asking how many of Ali's punches could a wrestler take in order to get close enough to grapple the boxer to the canvas. For a top competitor, history shows that the answer is probably 'enough'.

Nineteenth-century heavyweight boxing champions Bob Fitzsimmons and John L. Sullivan both lost impromptu bouts to wrestlers in short order. By the 1960s it was time that a proper controlled contest was held under specific rules. In August 1963, an article appeared in the soft-porn magazine *Rogue* in which the boxing enthusiast Jim Beck threw down a $1,000 challenge: 'Judo bums hear me one and all! It is one thing to fracture pine boards, bricks, and assorted inanimate objects, but quite another to climb into a ring with a trained and less cooperative target. My money is ready. Where are the takers?' First up was judo champion Gene LeBell, a close friend and training partner of Bruce Lee himself. Facing a middleweight contender, LeBell choked Beck's representative unconscious in the fourth round.

Recent history is even more telling, as now there's an arena in which the different fighting styles can be directly compared: the Ultimate Fighting Championship. Almost anything goes in mixed martial arts, or 'cage fighting', except for eye gouging and blows to the groin. Yet, contrary to the public's expectation when the sport began, kung fu masters have fared notably badly – even worse than pure boxers. The early years were dominated by grapplers, and even today fighters stand little chance unless they have excellent wrestling skills as so many matches are settled on the ground, either with a submission hold or with one protagonist pinned down and pummelled unconscious.

The most successful mixed martial artist of recent times is Japan's Kazushi Sakuraba. Sakuraba came from professional (that is to say, staged) wrestling, but after his promoters went bust he talked his way into the Ultimate Fighting Championship's heavyweights-only Ultimate Japan tournament in 1997. He pretended that he weighed 203 pounds in order to qualify and, although he was really only 183 pounds, he defeated a 243-pound jiu-jitsu champion to score the first of several victories against bigger, stronger men. One of his smaller victims was the renowned Royce Gracie, who at 180 pounds himself once beat a 275-pound heavyweight wrestler. Sakuraba's career and those of other champions in Ultimate Fighting appear to demonstrate that grappling skills are far more effective than other martial arts or boxing disciplines in overcoming a size disadvantage. The UFC has destroyed the mystique of martial arts by showing which techniques actually work. Kung fu is not one of them.

Bruce Lee had great respect for the skills of wrestlers, but he had different priorities and recognized that their techniques were not as photogenic as the looping kicks and acrobatics that moviegoers wanted to see. He realized that his moves were only for the camera, and that the flurries of hand trapping that he learned from wing chun kung fu would be of little use in a real fight. Unlike Ali, Lee never boasted that he could take on the world. Unlike Chuck Norris, he never fought in competitive tournaments either. To then say that Lee was the best martial arts fighter in the world – let alone the best fighter per se – would be like saying that the Harlem Globetrotters, basketball's answer to the WWF, are the world's best basketball team. The more valid question is not whether Bruce Lee could beat Muhammad Ali, but how he would fare against Rocky Balboa...

What is the most dangerous sport?

Contrary to popular belief, the vogue for extreme sports did not begin in the United States but at England's Oxford University in the mid-seventies, when David Kirke, Chris Baker and Ed Hulton set up the notorious Dangerous Sports Club. It was Kirke who invented modern bungee jumping in 1979, when he tied a rubber cord to his ankles and jumped off the Clifton Suspension Bridge, for which he was arrested and fined £100 for breaching the peace. The stunt was based on the Pentecost Island tradition of 'land jumping', in which tribesmen tie themselves to vines and then dive headfirst into sand from 80-foot wooden towers. The most famous member of the club was Monty's Python's Graham Chapman, whose contributions included riding a gondola down a ski run and being thrown through the air over London's Hyde Park by a machine used to launch fighter jets from aircraft carriers. Since then the club has pioneered activities such as BASE jumping – parachuting from Buildings, Antennas, Spans (bridges) and Earth (cliffs) – launching people from giant catapults, zorbing (rolling down mountains inside inflated plastic spheres) and hang-gliding over active volcanoes. It is no wonder that their emblem was a wheelchair, or that they were eventually banned by college authorities.

But for those extreme sports enthusiasts jaded by

volcanoes and cliff tops, all they need do to restore their adrenaline flow is put on a pair of trunks because, at first glance, swimming is far and away the most dangerous sporting activity for adults in the United Kingdom. A study by Dr David Ball of Middlesex University showed that between 1988 and 1992, 315 out of 708 sporting fatalities in the UK (or 44 per cent) were from drowning.[74] Second place was taken by motor sports, with sixty-five deaths, closely followed by horse riding with sixty-two. Side by side in fourth were mountain climbing and air sports, including hang-gliding, paragliding, parachuting and flying light aircraft, with fifty-one deaths. In sixth – just when you thought it was safe to go back to the water – were non-drowning accidents from all water sports, including swimming, which accounted for forty-nine fatalities.

However, the average adult swims on eight occasions each year, but only indulges in a motorcycle race or rally car trial 0.3 times a year. To get a true sense of the danger involved, we must multiply the fatalities in the latter by 26.7 to achieve parity. The result is that if we had spent as much time on the racetrack as in the swimming pool, there would be 1,736 fewer of us living to tell the tale. The world's most dangerous single sporting event is the 10,000-kilometre, sixteen-day Paris–Dakar Rally, which has on average claimed the lives of two competitors each year, along with an unknown number of spectators. Admittedly, drivers face sandstorms, bandits, rebel armies and landmines in addition to the breakneck speeds involved. Giving the same comparative treatment to other sports means we could expect 620 deaths each year from horse riding, 1,020 from climbing and a monstrous 13,600 from air sports.[75] And most of those poor hang-gliders and parachutists would not be going out of their way to involve active volcanoes and giant catapults in their plans.

With the exception of air sports, and sometimes of horse riding, mountain climbing and motor racing, we do not undertake sport with any expectation that we might die in the process. On average, 163 people die in sporting accidents each year,[76] which is a low figure when put into context: in 1992 alone, there were 4,628 deaths on the roads, 4,521 in the home and 400 in the workplace. Most of us are more concerned with the possibility of injury. And so we should be, because every year four million Britons take time off sick after playing sport.[77] Playing football results in around 250,000 visits to A & E each year, but as with swimming fatalities, this does not make it the most dangerous sport for injuries. Comparing the number of attendances at hospital Accident and Emergency departments in 1992 against participation rates, rugby is more than twice as risky, with 440 attendances per 100,000 adult participations. Soccer comes second with 200, followed by cricket, hockey and skiing, which account for 130 each, then netball, with eighty-two attendances. Motor racing, which kills sixty-five each year, ranks a modest eighth, with fifty-eight attendances. Horse riding seems even safer in eleventh place with twenty-six. Mountain climbing is a walk in the park in twelfth place on seventeen attendances – barely more dangerous than tennis, which suffers fifteen. Of course, if your safety line fails at 3,000 feet then you will not make it as far as Casualty.

Rugby seems to be less dangerous in other parts of the world. In Australia, for example, Aussie Rules football tops the list for injuries with, according to Dr Peter Larkins, a contributor to the Medibank Private Safe Sports Report in 2006, around 14,200 amateur players being injured every day.[78] This makes Aussie Rules much more dangerous than rugby league or union, which were rated only ninth and tenth, exceeded by basketball, netball, cricket and even aerobics.

In the United States, American football garners the most injuries, but when participation rates are considered it is easily outstripped by an unlikely rival. More than half the total injuries sustained by female athletes in American high schools and colleges are the result of over-enthusiastic cheerleading celebrations. According to the US National Center for Catastrophic Sports Injury Research, cheerleading accounts for more cases of 'catastrophic' injuries such as spinal and head trauma than all other sports combined. Human pyramids have recently been limited to 2.5 body lengths in colleges because so many young women were hurting themselves in falls. Most dangerous of all moves is the 'basket throw', in which a cheerleader is propelled up to 20 feet in the air by the locked arms of her colleagues. Unfortunately, arms have a tendency to become unlocked at the wrong moment. Even worse, the 'flier' sometimes ends up catapulted over their shoulders on to a hard surface.

Since the early nineties, injuries sustained during cheerleading have more than doubled – from 12,000 in 1991 to 28,000 in 2004. Cheerleading has become more acrobatic as it has attracted girls who would once have expended their energies on gymnastics. Natural gymnasts have been frustrated in recent years as the sport has been curtailed because educational authorities can no longer afford the expensive lawsuits that follow serious injuries. Today, the process has begun to repeat itself. The National Collegiate Athletic Association's Catastrophic Injury Insurance Program reports that 25 per cent of money spent on claims since 1998 has gone to cheerleaders. This makes it second only to gridiron as a source of claims, yet the ratio of college football players to cheerleaders is around 100 to 12.[79]

According to health agencies today, the only thing more dangerous than cheerleading, rugby or even joining the Dangerous Sports Club is to do no sport at all. If you really want to risk your life, then you can do no better than sitting on a couch eating crisps for several years. Obesity is roundly agreed to be the new smoking, and our appetite for junk food and distaste for physical exertion is set to result in the first fall in life expectancy across the civilized world since the end of the Second World War. The risk of suffering ill health from physical exercise pales by comparison.

Why does sport favour left-handers?

Pelé, Diego Maradona, Johan Cruyff, Brian Lara, David Gower, John McEnroe, Martina Navratilova, Babe Ruth. Along with 10 per cent of the world's population, all these sporting greats had one thing in common: they are or were left-handed. Professional sport seems to be biased in favour of lefties. This is most pronounced in fencing, where they currently make up over 40 per cent of top-class competitors. It is also significant in boxing, cricket, judo, karate, tennis and table tennis, where over twice as many left-handers make it to the top as one would expect from their incidence in the population at large. These are all confrontational sports, and no such effect is observed in running, skiing, swimming, rowing or other activities in which competitors do not form part of the playing space.[80]

There is some evidence that left-handers enjoy innate advantages over their peers. In 2006, a study at the Australian National University discovered that left-handers think more quickly when playing computer games and sports.[81] The connections between their left and right brain hemispheres were faster than those of right-handed subjects, and they found it easier to use the whole brain to work on a task. 'Extreme' left-handed volunteers were up to 43 milliseconds faster in completing spatial tests. But this disparity is not enough to account for the success of left-handed sportsmen and -women, since they do not excel in those events that are most purely a matter of hand-eye coordination or reaction times, such as darts or goalkeeping.

In some cases, the structure of a given sport mitigates in favour of left-handedness. For example, in baseball a left-handed hitter stands on the right side of the plate, meaning that he will begin his run around three feet closer to first base. It might seem that this should be counteracted because the hitter will have his back to the direction in which he will have to run, whereas right-handers face straight ahead. However, the hitter's body spins round as he completes his swing, meaning that this factor is actually a further advantage for the left-handed hitter. The direction they face also gives an advantage to left-handed pitchers, who can spot base-stealing attempts since they naturally face first base.

In cricket, left-handed spin bowlers can direct the ball into the rough patches created by the fast bowlers on the other side of the wicket. A cricket team can tire out an opposing side by playing one right- and one left-handed batsman, forcing the fielders to rearrange their positions each time the batsmen change ends. It is also argued that left-handed batsmen profit from confusing umpires about the line of leg stump, so that they are sometimes given the benefit of the doubt when they look to be out from other angles.

For the most part, however, the explanation for lefties' success is the very fact that they are in a minority. Non-English-speaking southpaws sometimes complain that words in their languages associated with 'left' have acquired negative connotations in the English language, giving us terms such as 'gauche,' 'maladroit' and 'sinister'. Left-handedness has been connected with every ailment from mental illness to low life-expectancy. According to Charlotte Faurie and Michel Raymond of the Paris Institute of Evolutionary Sciences, the reason for the lefty's advantage in sport – and the continued existence of lefties in the gene pool at all – is indeed quite sinister.

Faurie and Raymond discovered that the murder rate is higher in those tribal societies that have more left-handers than others (tribal societies were chosen for their study since the weapons of choice were less likely to be guns, where handedness is irrelevant). They reasoned that since the left-handed assailant's opponent would be more used to facing right-handed opponents, his attack would be more likely to be successful. The same rationale, the so-called 'fight hypothesis', follows for why left-handers have an advantage in certain sports – those where one-on-one confrontations occur.[82] In fencing, seven of the top sixteen competitors in the world are left-handed, having reached their position by beating predominantly right-handed opponents. The French neuroscientist Guy Azemar examined the proportion of left-handers in international championships over several years.[83] He found that around a third of top fencers are left-handed, including the Italian Edoardo Mangiarotti, the greatest ever fencer and winner of six Olympic gold medals. Mangiarotti was born right-handed but was forced by his father to fence with his left in order to gain an advantage.

The same consideration helps explain why the last three world record holders for the most runs in a Test match are all left-handed: Matthew Hayden, Brian Lara and Sir Garfield Sobers. The top teams in general have a preponderance of left-handed batsmen. A study of the 2003 cricket World Cup revealed that of the 177 players who batted in the tournament, a quarter were lefties, including nearly half those making up the first three places in their team's order. The winning team, Australia, boasted four lefties out of its top six batsmen.

Professional tennis players train themselves to place the ball on the opponent's backhand, which will normally be their weaker stroke. When they face left-handed opponents, their muscle memory is frustrated as they find themselves having to do the opposite. However, as more left-handers are found in the upper echelons of the sport, players presumably become more used to playing them, so there is an upper limit to the advantage. In practice, lefties make up around twice as many top tennis players than their 'rightful share'.

In basketball, defensive positions favour left-handers because, as Bill Russell explained in his autobiography *Second Wind*,[84] 'your stronger and surer hand is always opposite the shooting hand of the player you're guarding'. By the same principle, lefties are at a disadvantage when it comes to offence, which is why they have been very scarce in the ranks of the highest scorers in recent years.

Perhaps the greatest example of the advantage of unfamiliarity is the world record-breaking boxing match between Mike Collins and Pat Brownson on 4 November 1947. The left-handed Collins took up a conventional right-handed stance as the fight began but then switched his posture and delivered a left-hook, knocking out his opponent after just four seconds. However, there is one sport where left-handers will never best their rivals. In 1975, polo's authorities prohibited wielding the mallet in one's left hand for reasons of safety.

Why do female tennis players earn more than the men?

Before February 2007, when 'equal' pay for both sexes was finally instigated at Wimbledon – the last of the grand slams to hold out – this question was asked the other way around. Women started competing at Wimbledon in 1884. That year, the women's singles champion was awarded a silver flower basket worth 20 guineas while the men's winner walked away with a 30-guinea gold trophy. At the All England Club's first Open championship in 1968, when professionals were allowed to compete, Billie Jean King won £750 compared to Rod Laver's £2,000. By 2006, however, the gap had closed to the point where Amelie Mauresmo won only £30,000 less than Roger Federer's £655,000. But the authorities had never allowed full parity on a point of principle. Men's matches are far longer, going to the best of five sets rather than three. This gives women more time to play doubles and mixed doubles games, with the result that the best of them were already earning more from the tournament than the strongest male players.

As the All England Club chairman Tim Phillips put it in 2006: 'This issue is one of a judgement on fairness. We believe that what we do at the moment is actually fair to the men as well as to the women. It just doesn't seem right to us that the lady players could play in three events and could take away significantly more than the men's champion who battles away through these best-of-five matches. We also would point out that the top ten ladies last year earned more from Wimbledon than the top ten men did... We could respond to the pressures and do something that would be fundamentally unfair to the men, but we have not.'[85] This proved to be a final act of defiance after years of politically correct obloquy, and a year later he made an ignominious U-turn. Through gritted teeth he explained: 'Tennis is one of the few sports in which women and men compete in the same event at the same time. We believe our decision to offer equal prize-money provides a boost for the game as a whole and recognizes the enormous contribution that women players make to the game and to Wimbledon.'[86]

The All England Club may have changed its mind, but this does not change the facts of the matter. Mr Phillips had not even brought up the far greater sums female players can make through sponsorship deals. In 2006, endorsements helped Maria Sharapova reach number sixty-three in *Forbes* magazine's list of 100 Most Powerful Celebrities after earning $19 million. Serena and Venus Williams were at numbers 87 and 90 respectively, with no male player anywhere to be seen. Even with unequal prize money, women players were paid more per game than men at the 2005 tournament. The last eight players in the women's singles took home an average £1,432 for every game they played, while the men were paid £993 per game. Because the women were able to play in the doubles and mixed doubles, their top ten earned 4 per cent more prize money than the top ten men. If every match ends in straight sets, then by the end of Wimbledon fortnight the men's champion will have played 50 per cent more sets than his female counterpart. This would rise to 67 per cent if every match were to go the distance. In 2006,

Roger Federer had to play 202 games in order to win the men's singles title, whereas Amelie Mauresmo played only 142. Despite doing 42 per cent more work, Federer received only 5 per cent more prize money.

Those who make this argument are guilty not of chauvinism, but of economic naivety. If everyone were to be paid a rate based on how long and hard they work, we would not be living in a capitalist system and it would be very unlikely that Wimbledon would even exist. In a capitalist economy, wages are based not upon moral desserts or the supposed innate value of your labour, but on the market's demand for one's services. In this case, it is neither here nor there whether women play three sets, five sets or just one set. All that matters is what people are prepared to pay to watch their matches and what sponsors are willing to spend to secure advertising slots during their breaks.

Historically, the All England Club has maintained that spectators generally prefer the men's game. Surveys have consistently shown that roughly 70 per cent of tennis fans concur.[87] Firms sometimes charge up to twice as much for corporate hospitality at men's ties, and there are more commercial breaks generating extra revenue in a long drawn out five-and-a-half-hour men's game. But in 2005, 6.8 million television viewers watched the ladies' final, whereas the men's attracted only 5.8 million. Women's tennis is enjoying a surge in popularity due to the glamour of several top competitors and the predictability of the men's contest. In the dull days of Pete Sampras and Jim Courier, they did not even need glamour to be more popular than the men.

If a revolution should one day sweep all this away, the chauvinist argument would be no stronger, and not just because tennis players could no longer expect to be paid at all merely for enjoying themselves in the sun. If men were to be paid more than women on the basis that they play more sets, then this would mean that they should have an amount deducted from their pay packets whenever a player wins a match 3-0. And should they receive a bonus for long tie-breaks? The rules of baseball were once changed to prevent players from conspiring to prolong series games and thereby boost their salaries. A system based on supposed fairness would be open to abuse and arcane to the point of ridiculousness. There is, of course, a far simpler solution. Women have not always played just three sets. In the nineteenth century they played five until, according to legend, a woman who insisted on wearing a corset during a match fainted and the rules were changed. Martina Navratilova once offered to return to the original system in return for equal pay, but her request was turned down. The authorities ought to reconsider.

Does the jockey matter?

American jockeys tell an apocryphal story about a race in the thirties involving the jockeys Johnny Adams and Silvio Coucci. Their mounts were neck and neck when Coucci dropped his whip going into the final straight. He looked over to his rival, cursed and said, 'I'd beat you if I hadn't lost my whip', upon which Adams handed over his own before taking the reins in both hands and going on to win the race. The tale is intended to demonstrate the relative talents of the two protagonists, but if true it probably happened because Adams' mount was the superior beast. No authority on the turf would deny that a horse is more important than its rider to the outcome of a race.

The part the jockey does have to play is by turns significant and exaggerated. The jockeys' leader board gives a misleading impression of the relative merits of each rider. The championship itself has become a self-fulfilling prophecy in which the jockey perceived to be the best is given the best mounts, leading to more wins and an enhanced perception that he is the best.

This is not to underestimate the difficulties of the jockey's art. They have to pilot an animal weighing upwards of 1,000 pounds around a track and sometimes over tall hedges at up to 40 mph. They must have the nerve to go for a gap between two other mountains of horseflesh travelling at the same speed. According to the jump jockey Guy Lewis, the effort is equivalent to running an 800 metres race – and they have to do it several times in an afternoon.[88] He or she has to do all this in various states of starvation. Champion jump jockey Tony McCoy has ridden two stone under his natural weight, while Lester Piggott would drive to mid-August race meetings wearing a sweat-suit with the heater on full to keep his weight down to eight stone. Fred Archer, the greatest jockey of the nineteenth century, shot himself in a delirium brought on by fasting. Malnutrition is not the only danger. According to the Jockey Club, one in fourteen steeplechase rides results in a fall, and one in eighty in an injury. There were seven deaths in British racing between 1980 and 2000. Yet few National Hunt jockeys make a decent living, and some even make a loss after equipment and transport costs have been deducted.

Some thoroughbreds are extremely wilful and need a firm or familiar rider to control them. Colin Brown, Desert Orchid's regular rider from 1983 to 1988, remembers how 'Once he strengthened up, you could do whatever you wanted on him. It was like driving a Ferrari rather than a Cortina... Basically all I had to do most of the time was just sit on him.'[89] It was not always thus. For example, Simon Sherwood, Dessie's most successful rider by win-rate, once had to pull the horse off his stride momentarily as the grey almost barged his rival Yahoo into the rails on the way to winning the Cheltenham Gold Cup in 1989.[90]

It's when a horse wishes to run away with a rider that the jockey earns his or her pay. All horses have a final sprinting distance, and a jockey needs to be able to gauge when to begin that sprint. Knowing precisely when to hold a horse back and when to let it run free can make the difference between keeping the right pace for a fast finish and burning a horse out. This ability improves with experience, but it has taken on mythic proportions in the minds of racegoers and professionals alike.

There is a popular belief that some jockeys have a Dr Doolittle-esque ability to understand a horse and coax extraordinary performances out of ordinary animals. But no jockey can make a horse go faster than it is capable of running. On 28 December 1996, Frankie Dettori rode all seven winners on the race card at Ascot, prompting the sportswriter Simon Barnes to later comment:

> My own contribution to the debate concerns the galvanizing communication between horse and rider. It is the exact corollary of the truth that horses know when the rider is nervous... Fujiyama Crest certainly sensed Dettori's supreme confidence, and if that sort of thing doesn't affect a horse's performance, then I've never patted a horse in my life. 'He'd have won on a seaside donkey in the last,' said former champion jockey John Francombe... 'We've all had that Frankie experience – even if it lasts for only ten minutes. They don't come very often, but at least in sport we can experience them vicariously.' [91]

John Francombe was obviously exaggerating, but Barnes was mistaken if he thinks the feat had anything to do with 'galvanizing communications'. Given the number of jockeys riding every working day, year in year out, it would be more surprising if no one ever swept a race card. Dettori's achievement, while unique in British racing, is nothing more than what a statistician would expect to occur sooner or later with or without any 'supreme confidence'.

The more a game depends upon skill, the more often one would expect to see the same faces winning tournaments. Similarly, games that depend mostly upon luck throw up more random champions. Backgammon, for example, has found a different world champion every year bar one since the inception of the event in Monte Carlo in 1975. On that basis, horseracing would seem to be somewhere towards the other end of the skill/luck axis as its history shows certain individuals dominating for several seasons at a time. Between 1981 and 2007, only four men have held the title of National Hunt Champion Jockey. In the twenty-nine years between 1925 and 1953, Sir Gordon Richards was Flat Race Champion Jockey twenty-six times. Nevertheless, such runs aren't all down to superior skill.

A good jockey is often one who makes fewer mistakes rather than one who coaxes an extraordinary performance out of his horse. In this case, the best or most reliable riders should show better results than their rivals when all considered are riding a 'sure thing'. Out of the twenty-nine jockeys who rode more than twenty odds-on favourites between 1993 and July 2000, Frankie Dettori scored a healthy 155 wins from 249 rides, or 62.25 per cent, but this was only enough to put him in sixth place. The best record belonged to Seb Sanders, with thirty wins from thirty-nine rides, or 78.95 per cent. Tony McGlone had the worst record, with fifteen wins out of thirty-three rides, or just 45.45 per cent. Before McGlone, in twenty-eighth position, was

Kevin Darley with 108 wins out of 198 rides, or 54.55 per cent. From these statistics, a lay observer would imagine Darley's horsemanship to be extremely poor given the regularity with which he snatched defeat from the jaws of victory. Far from it: in 2000, Darley was crowned Champion Jockey and was regarded, perhaps mistakenly as it turns out, as one of the safest pairs of hands in racing.

Former champions Pat Eddery and Willie Carson also find themselves in the bottom half of the table. Eleven-time champion Eddery recorded 161 wins, which was more than anyone else managed, and this helped him to win two championships in the period. On the other hand, no one else apart from Frankie Dettori had nearly so many rides. Eddery secured a massive haul of 274 odds-on mounts, but he does not seem to have served them particularly well at seventeenth place in the table and a modest win-rate of 58.76 per cent. A variation of 33.53 per cent between Sanders and McGlone, the best and worst performing subjects in the study, points to a significant role for the skill of the jockey in racing. But the figures also show that that skill is easily passed over or distorted due to the way the championship is decided by aggregate wins rather than win/loss ratio.[92]

Another indicator beloved of punters is how much profit or loss one would show by betting on a jockey's every mount during a season. Running the numbers yields some startling results. Since the mid-nineties, Ireland's Tony McCoy has been the dominant rider over the jumps, with twelve consecutive championships between 1996 and 2007. He was the fastest ever jockey to 1,000 winners and holds the record for the most winners in a season: 289 during 2001–2. His achievements make him the greatest jockey in National Hunt history. Now compare the all-conquering McCoy to Swindon's Wayne Hutchinson. In the five seasons starting 2002–3, McCoy rode 1,029 winners – over five times as many as Hutchinson's 191. And lest this be put down to McCoy's greater number of mounts – 4,047 compared with his rival's 1,635 – his record gives him a handsome win-rate of 25 per cent while Hutchinson languishes on just under 12 per cent. It is no wonder that McCoy's position at the top of the jockeys' leader-board was unassailable, while Hutchinson managed to place only 26th, 49th, 28th, 18th and 13th. However, these figures do not look so impressive when we build in the added value each jockey gives to his mount, for the supposed journeyman has done a far better job of beating the odds. A punter making a £1 wager on each of McCoy's rides during this period would be irked to find himself £471.31 out of pocket. The same amount wagered on Hutchinson would yield a £77.71 profit. Not much perhaps, but then horse racing is a mug's game after all.[93]

Why is baseball's World Series so named when only North American teams take part?

According to European prejudice, baseball's World Series is so called because Americans simply don't realize that the rest of the world exists. Americans are quick to counter with the 'real' story, which is that the name has nothing to do with patriotic arrogance and stems simply from a former sponsor of the event: the *New York World* newspaper, and shame on those knee-jerk anti-Americans for thinking otherwise. Unfortunately, the *New York World* never sponsored the World Series. The Europeans' suspicion, it turns out, is quite accurate.

In the 1880s the term 'World Championship Series' was first used for the post-season play-off between the champions of the National League and the American Association. It was at the time fair, albeit overblown, to describe the winners as 'world champions' since the game was only played to a high standard in one country. The phrase 'World Series' soon stuck, and since then sponsors and reporters have seen no reason to change it. Many baseball fans still think of the winners as the true world champions, and victorious players often describe themselves as such in post-game interviews. England felt the same way about football in the early twentieth century – until defeat by the USA in their first World Cup put paid to such arrogance. Indeed, the European club championship was invented by Frenchman Gabriel Hanot precisely as a means of proving that the best team in England was *not* the best in the world, as Stan Cullis claimed, after his Wolverhampton Wanderers side beat Hungary's Honved in a friendly in 1953.

It should be no surprise if the sporting ambitions of the world's only superpower meet the same fate as those of her imperial predecessor. US teams have hardly excelled in international competition. In mitigation, Major League players do not feature in the Olympic Games since they clash with the home season. The college athletes and Minor League players sent in their place have won at one of the four Games held since 1992. The Cuban team won the other three. The Baseball World Cup is held every two years, but until 1996 it was limited to amateur entrants, and after 1996 Major League teams would not allow their employees to play in the competition. Since 1938, the USA has won only twice – in 1973 and 1974. The most successful side has been Cuba with twenty-five victories. However, in 2006 a rival to the World Cup was created by the Major League Baseball authorities themselves: the World Baseball Classic, in which America's finest players could take part. In the inaugural event, Team USA struggled against Mexico before being knocked out in the second round by Japan.

Do teams wearing red really do better?

In 1964, Liverpool were due to face Anderlecht in the second-round tie of their first ever season in Europe. Eager to win the psychological battle, manager Bill Shankly hit on the idea of an all-red strip that would make his giant Scots defender Ron 'the Colossus' Yeats even more intimidating on the pitch. Shankly produced a pair of red shorts to match the team jersey and the centre forward Ian St John suggested red socks to complete the new outfit. Shankly was pleased with his handiwork. 'Christ, Ronnie,' he said, 'you look awesome, terrifying. You look seven feet tall.' Anderlecht duly wilted and the Reds won 4-0 on aggregate.

Is it just a coincidence that English football's three most successful teams – Liverpool, Manchester United and Arsenal – all play in red, or does the colour really boost performance and rattle the opposition? After all, the similarly attired Belgium and Poland have hardly fared well in the World Cup over the years – even if England's crowning moment on that stage came when wearing blood red rather than white. Statistics show that in Euro 2004, wearing predominantly red was worth an extra goal a game on average. At the very least, players find scarlet-clad colleagues easier to pick out against the green of a pitch – unlike Manchester United's infamous grey strip that was blamed for a poor run of form.

Robert Barton and Robert Hill at Durham University also investigated contests in tae kwon do, boxing and Graeco-Roman and freestyle wrestling from the 2004 Olympics.[94] These were sports in which the colours red and blue were randomly assigned to competitors. In all four sports, red won the most bouts – 55 per cent overall. This advantage rose to 62 per cent in contests between competitors that experts judged to be evenly matched. However, simply wearing red cannot turn anyone into a good competitor. The researchers speculate that red is the colour that signifies male dominance and high testosterone in primates and other animals. For example, among troops of mandrill apes the dominant males will have redder faces and buttocks than less successful rivals. As they age and their testosterone levels decline, they begin to lose their pigmentation. With red being the colour of anger, it is not absurd to expect it to be the colour of intimidation. Barton suggested accordingly that wearing red might give a sportsman a testosterone surge, while having the opposite effect on his opponents.

Red is not the only colour to make a difference to performance on the field. Between 1970 and 1986, the black-clad Los Angeles Raiders led the NFL in number of yards penalized, while the similarly attired Philadelphia Flyers were penalized for more minutes than any other team in the National Hockey League. Two hockey teams, the Pittsburgh Penguins and the Vancouver Canucks, found their disciplinary records deteriorating when they swapped from white to black uniforms. Research suggests both that black clothing incites players to worse behaviour and that the same infraction is viewed as slightly more grievous in the eyes of witnesses when the perpetrator is wearing dark clothing. Perhaps years of black-clad

Hollywood villains have warped our expectations.[95] It is a testament to New Zealand's rugby players that most All Blacks teams over the years have nevertheless kept a clean reputation.

Football referees might suffer less abuse if they abolished black uniforms, but it is unlikely to happen. Neither will more teams switch their home colours to red. Former Leicester City captain Matt Elliott has commented, without irony, 'I think this is a load of old rubbish. We never felt we were disadvantaged by wearing blue.' Clearly the explanation lies elsewhere.

Why does the England football team underachieve?

According to former England manager Graham Taylor, 'We expect to win big tournaments but I don't know why. I don't really know where that expectation comes from. We've won one World Cup since it began in 1930, and that was forty-one years ago and at home. Why people expect England to win big tournaments every two years, in the heat of summer, is beyond me. We're a quarter-final team, not a genuine world force.'[96] This shows a lack of understanding of the average fan. Apart from an over-hyped aberration in 2006, the English public have not seriously expected their team to win the World Cup since 1970. What the fans do expect is for their team to play *well* or, failing that, with passion. This is why Owen Hargreaves became so popular despite England's woeful performances in Germany in 2006. And it is why few neutrals were impressed when the team beat their Teutonic archrivals 1-0 in Euro 2000, which one pundit described as 'like watching two fat drunks slug it out in a pub car park'.

No one blames the manager if the team loses due to bad luck or despite a valiant effort. What drives the fans and the media to rage against the manager is when his team deserves to lose. As for the summer sun, English footballers may play most of their season in cold conditions, but Germany is hardly a tropical paradise either and this has not affected that country's national side. Neither is it just the lack of success in big tournaments that irks the fans, for the team has a history of poor displays against the weakest nations in football. During the European Championship qualifier against Andorra in March 2007, spectators were so incensed that their stars could not score against the team ranked 163rd in the world that England's substitutes had to be moved from the stand to the dressing room for their own safety at half-time.

With so many first-rate players failing to reproduce their club form in an England shirt, the average hard-working fan can hardly be blamed for putting the shortfall down to moral turpitude. In today's Premiership of inflated salaries and playboy lifestyles, English players may well be lazy, pampered and overpaid. But this hardly sets them apart from their foreign counterparts. Indeed, in terms of the number of matches they play in a season, England's footballers are paragons of industry. The following table gives the first team appearances made by outfield players at club level for the season preceding the 2006 World Cup:

*England**		*Italy*	
John Terry	50	Vincenzo Iaquinta	33
Rio Ferdinand	52	Gianluca Zambrotta	40
Jamie Carragher	58	Fabio Cannavaro	45
Steven Gerrard	53	Marco Materazzi	31
Owen Hargreaves	19	Andrea Pirlo	32
Frank Lampard	50	Gennaro Gattuso	46
Joe Cole	48	Fabio Grosso	41
David Beckham	38	Simone Perrotta	42

| Wayne Rooney | 48 | Francesco Totti | 26 |
| Peter Crouch | 49 | Luca Toni | 38 |

*Ashley Cole and Michael Owen are not included because they spent the majority of the 2005/6 season out injured.

The English players had on average played forty-seven domestic games over the season compared to just thirty-seven for the Italians. Frank Lampard, much maligned for his poor form in Germany, had played 35 per cent more games than the average Italian playing for the tournament-winning side – in other words, his average rival's season ended over three months earlier than his own. England's stars were unable to match their club form because they were exhausted, and they were exhausted precisely because their club form had been so good. It is also little wonder that Owen Hargreaves was England's most energetic player by far, having played just nineteen times for Bayern Munich.

It's also tempting (for England managers, very tempting) to blame failure on simple bad luck. Bad luck and injuries to key players have occurred at the worst moments. Alf Ramsey could curse the Mexican water supply that gave Gordon Banks gastroenteritis in 1970. Kevin Keegan and Trevor Brooking were unable to participate in the 1982 World Cup until the very end of England's run. Bryan Robson was rarely available when he was needed most, while the team's three best players of recent years – Wayne Rooney, Michael Owen and David Beckham – have all been crocked either during or in the lead-up to World Cups. England have also won just one penalty shoot-out in seven attempts. But thinking of penalties as a matter of luck has been part of the problem. The belief has led certain managers of the national side to neglect to practise shoot-outs before major tournaments. Bad luck has been less influential at times than the poor leadership the team has suffered.

Similarly, injuries ought not to matter as much to England as to other nations, because the country has a reasonably large population and a strong professional league that should offer a wealth of options in every position. However, in recent years England managers have had fewer and fewer top-flight players to choose from. Out of twenty Premiership clubs in the 2006–7 season, only six fielded an Englishman as their first-choice goalkeeper (Tottenham's Paul Robinson, Portsmouth's David James, West Ham's Robert Green, Charlton's Scott Carson, Wigan's Chris Kirkland and Watford's Ben Foster). There were almost as many Americans plying their trade in goal: Blackburn's Brad Friedel, Everton's Tim Howard and Reading's Marcus Hahnemann. In February 2007, only 40 per cent of Premiership players were English, compared with 72.5 per cent of Serie A players who were Italian.[97] Given the vast resources available to many English clubs, it is a wonder that even this many get the chance to enjoy first team football. It is not just the top stars who keep promising English youngsters off the field. Pound for pound, foreign players represent better value for money. For example, Nemanja Vidic is widely regarded as the equal of Rio Ferdinand in the centre of Manchester United's defence, yet while Ferdinand was a record-breaking £30 million purchase, Vidic was picked up from Spartak Moscow for £7.5 million. The Premiership would be virtually all foreign were the clubs more knowledgeable about young talent abroad. But to blame the influx of foreign players on England's poor form is simply wrong: the rot had already set in long before then. Here we get to the crux of the problem, which is the deficit of skill.

Part of the problem goes beyond football. Sir Trevor Brooking, now the FA's Director of Football Development, points to 'a worrying statistic from the Department of Education Inspectorate that 60 per cent of all our 11-year-olds leaving primary school are physically illiterate. This means that they do not possess the basic ABC of physical movement which are agility, balance and coordination.'[98] For a number of reasons, from their love of PlayStations to their parents' fear of paedophiles, children in England are spending less and less of their time outdoors perfecting their sporting prowess. When youngsters do venture out, they find there are few places for them to go. England is a very urban country – its population density is the highest in the world after Japan and the Netherlands and stands at eight times that of the United States. As the number of cars on the roads has steadily increased, the number of spots safe for street football has diminished. This makes children dependent upon land set aside for sporting use. Yet great swathes of school playing fields were sold off in the eighties as local governments saw a means of raising funds and left-wing education authorities sought to crush competitive sports. Children, they thought, should never be declared losers. The result is that English adults are rarely winners.

Damien Comolli, the Sporting Director of Tottenham Hotspur, argues that the situation is exacerbated by the way young teenagers learn to play in England. 'Over four years between the ages of 12 and 16,' he told the BBC, 'a French boy would receive 2,304 hours of training. That is twice as much as England – where you would be given 1,152 hours. Those four years are crucial – they are the most important years in youth football – both physically and technically. It is difficult to catch up when you are 17 or 18.'[99] Comolli praises France, Holland and Portugal for their youth academies' emphasis on technique rather than competition.

Poor technique is almost a part of the English footballing tradition, shouldered aside by passion and commitment. But the British Isles have always produced skilful individuals, from Stanley Matthews to Glenn Hoddle and Paul Gascoigne. The nation's perennial weakness has been in bringing these talents together to sustain reliable passing movements and possession football. Gianluca Vialli has produced a new theory backed by his own research to explain this. His interest was sparked by Fabio Capello's report of a trip to Scotland:

> I worked with a Scottish youth side and had them do the same drills I would do in Italy. I realized that, between the wind, the rain, the cold, there was no way they could do it. How could you possibly teach somebody anything in those conditions? To me, it's obvious and it explains why Brazilians are more technical than Europeans... and, in Italy, the further south you go the more technical they are. You train better in good weather and the only way to become good is to train![100]

Vialli found that, contrary to popular belief, Northern Italy is colder and rainier than England during the months of the football season. Milan, for example, is far wetter than Manchester. However, a more important factor is that the wind blows 50 per cent faster in England. Arsene Wenger concurred:

'The wind ruins everything. It forces you to do only one type of exercise. It forces you to work on either speed or continuous movement. It's very rare that you get the chance to sit calmly and work on technique or tactics. You have to keep the players moving, otherwise they get cold.'[101]

Vialli recognizes that this still does not explain all the characteristics of English football. For instance, Britain's strong and unpredictable wind should militate against long-ball tactics and one might also wonder why the struggle to cope with windy conditions throughout their playing lifetimes does not make English players supremely skilful in their ball control and passing – rather like the advantage enjoyed by a marathon runner who trains at high altitude for an event at sea level. Perhaps this is simply not possible. A player, no matter how skilful, can only control the ball while he is in physical contact with it. Once it is away from his body, the elements take over.

In order to 'underachieve', the England team has to be pretty good in the first place, but the suspicion remains that the nation's stars are overrated. As Graham Taylor advises, perhaps the English should admit that their rightful place is well behind the other major footballing powers. And what else could one expect from a country that divides its attention between so many sports? The English should learn from the Australians, who limit themselves to cricket and rugby. Although they also do quite well at athletics of course. Oh, and swimming. And then they have entire leagues devoted to Aussie Rules football...

Why are Scorpios better at rugby than Leos?

'What is your star sign?' is not the most common ice-breaker at rugby club social gatherings. But perhaps it ought to be, as birth date has a significant influence on sporting ability. According to astrologers, Scorpios are determined, forceful and powerful, so maybe it is these qualities that help them to do so well in professional rugby. Librans and Sagittarians are also over-represented in international sides, as are Virgos born in September. But this is only among the northern nations. Scorpios lose their advantage south of the equator, where those born in the early months of the year seem to benefit instead. In fact, the effect has less to do with the vagaries of the planets than the iron law of the school calendar. In England, the school year begins in September, whereas in Australia, New Zealand and South Africa it starts at the end of January. Those born early in their school year have a greater chance of succeeding on the sports field than those born towards the end.

In England's rugby union squad for the summer of 2007, there were thirteen players born in the first three months of the school year and ten born in the last three months. Thus there were 30 per cent more 'early birds', as scientists refer to them. Looking to the southern hemisphere and the Australian and

Kiwi Union and League sides and the Springboks, the count was thirty-nine versus twenty-seven in total – a clear 44 per cent advantage in numbers for the early birds. Of these teams, only the All Blacks bucked the trend with more late-born players, yet their League countrymen more than made up for the deficit with four times as many early birds.

If your birthday falls in your country's summer, your chances of making the national team in a given sport are even slimmer than one would expect. The root of the injustice can be traced back to kindergarten, where there can be an age difference of almost an entire year between children in the same class. This gives the early birds a head start in mental and physical development that they can bring to bear in the sporting arena as well as in their studies. The effect knocks on through the grades, as early birds have their ability rewarded and reinforced with extra attention from PE teachers. They are more likely to be picked for school teams and then be noticed by regional sides. One would expect it to be greatest of all in rugby, where size and strength are so important, but it is just as influential in soccer. According to research carried out at Liverpool John Moores University, half of all England footballers who competed in international tournaments between 1986 and 1998 were born between September and December. Less than one in four were born between May and August.

A year is obviously significant for very young children – it represents a quarter of their entire life in pre-school after all – but educators used to think that the difference faded away as children entered their teens. This was why soccer players representing England at the schoolboy level so often failed to make it at the highest level – they had been picked for their size, which was no longer an advantage when their fellows caught up. However, the evidence suggests that the effect lingers into adulthood.

Can one swimming pool be 'faster' than another?

Everyone accepts that hi-tech running surfaces have helped track athletes to break world records, but to some it seems counterintuitive that similar developments could have helped swimmers. After all, it's only water, and H_2O is the same everywhere, isn't it? The brief history of the Homebush pool at Sydney International Aquatic Centre would perhaps suggest that there's more to it than that.

US$100 million went into creating the Homebush pool – and the money was not spent on the centre's aesthetics. New lane dividers were designed to reduce turbulence by containing each swimmer's backwash, creating what Australian coach Don Talbot described as 'millpond conditions' in each lane. Other measures reduce the waves that rebound from the walls and bottom of the pool, which is extra-wide, with ten lanes instead of the usual eight. The two lanes at the sides are the choppiest in a swimming pool, but they can be left empty in a top-class race at Homebush. The fastest qualifiers, of course, enjoy the privilege of the middle lanes where the water is calmest. The bottom is half a metre deeper than most other Olympic pools, meaning that less wave energy bounces back upwards to impede the swimmers. Even its shallowest point is 2.13 metres deep (7 feet). Like many pools today, the water level is kept to the brim, with a guttering system that sweeps away the wave tops before they can rebound. Even the starting blocks at Homebush are angled to allow faster starts, and adjacent handrails are now permitted for an extra push-off.

The benefits don't just stop there. The water in the pool is treated with ozone and ultraviolet light to reduce the need for chlorine. This means that there is two thirds less chlorine to irritate swimmers' mucous membranes or their eyes if it leaks into their goggles. The water temperature is 2° below that of the air. A fast pool should be slightly cold. If the water is kept at 25.5°C (78°F) then an athlete swimming at full speed will not overheat. Lower temperatures than this are counterproductive, as swimmers will feel stiff and their bodies will burn calories and waste energy heating themselves.

The result was that in August 1999, twelve world records were broken when Homebush hosted the Pan Pacific Championships. During the two months leading up to the 2000 Olympic Games, twenty world records were beaten there. At the Games themselves, fifteen world records were broken.

Is pregnancy a performance enhancer?

When the Scottish distance runner Liz McColgan became pregnant with her first child, she pulled on several pairs of tights to support her stomach and carried on training until two weeks before the happy event. She then rested for just two days before she returned to her regime. 'You feel really good, comfy and strong because you've got rid of all that weight,' she said. 'I felt fantastic after carrying the baby.'[102] Within a month she was running 90 miles a week and went on to win bronze in the 1990 World Cross Country Championships three months later and then gold in the World Championships of the same year.

McColgan is just one of many athletes who have found their best form after bearing children. Mother-of-two Fanny Blankers-Koen, the 'Flying Housewife', won four gold medals at the 1948 London Olympics. Norway's Ingrid Kristiansen won the Houston marathon five months after giving birth and recorded her personal best eighteen months later. In 1985 she won in London with a world record time of 2:21:06 – a feat not bettered until Paula Radcliffe's performance in 2002. Within two years she had also broken world records in the 5,000 metres and 10,000 metres. Russia's Svetlana Masterkova became a far superior athlete after giving birth to a daughter in the year before the 1996 Atlanta Olympics, where she won gold medals in the 800 metres and 1,500 metres. Later in the summer she broke the world record for the mile.

The body's various preparations for carrying a child and giving birth are known to enhance a woman's stamina and raise her hormone levels. This is partly because a woman's red blood cell count rises during the first three months of pregnancy. The increase in oxygen-carrying haemoglobin boosts heart and lung performance and, according to a study by the French sports medicine specialist Jean-Pierre de Mondenard, augments the muscles' capacity to use oxygen by up to 30 per cent.[103] Expectant mothers' higher levels of testosterone also aids their muscle strength, while extra progesterone makes the joints more flexible. Another study has even shown a 5 per cent increase in muscular efficiency during breastfeeding.[104]

For years it was rumoured that athletes in the Soviet bloc were obliged to become pregnant and then have abortions after two or three months as a form of 'natural' doping. In 1994 former gymnast Olga Kovalenko (née Karasseva) claimed on German television to have used the ploy shortly before her gold-medal-winning performance at the 1968 Olympic Games in Mexico and said that such tactics were common practice in the seventies, with 14-year-old girls forced to have sex with their coaches if they did not have a boyfriend.

However, better performances are not quite the norm. This is not because the physiological effects of pregnancy are erratic, though they can be, but because young children place demands on their parents that are not always compatible with the 100 per cent dedication that success at the highest levels of sport requires. Athletes in training need their sleep – something that is in short supply around a newborn baby.

Is there such a thing as a super-sub?

The original soccer 'super-sub' was Liverpool's flame-haired striker David Fairclough. During his debut season of 1975–6 he scored seven goals in fourteen games, and came off the bench in nine of them. In the quarter-final of the 1977 European Cup, Bob Paisley sent him on twenty minutes from time with Liverpool chasing a winning goal. When Fairclough poked the ball past the helpless St Etienne goalkeeper, the myth of the super-sub was born.

Kept out of Liverpool's formidable starting XI by the talents first of Kevin Keegan and John Toshack, then Kenny Dalglish and Ian Rush, Fairclough was forced to remain his manager Bob Paisley's 'secret weapon'. In the days when only a single substitution was allowed, the new man could make a disproportionate impact simply by being the only outfield player in the later stages of a game who wasn't exhausted. But fans have always believed that there is more to it than that. The super-sub, they believe, is a player who not only comes off the bench to score important goals late in a game, but is more likely to score them than if he'd started the match.

But why? Some fans claim that the super-sub can 'read' a game and, after studying the opposition and the movement of play for seventy minutes, can come on and score seemingly with his first touch. It was for this reason that former Chelsea manager Gianluca Vialli described the tall Norwegian forward Tore Andre Flo as 'the best player in the world when he comes off the bench'.[105] This was evidently not seen as a compliment as Flo left Chelsea after getting tired of warming the bench. Other pundits believe that super-subs are players who do not require a build-up, or need to get the measure of their marker before they can score. When two such contradictory explanations are offered, it's no surprise that there's something wrong with the whole notion of a super-sub. But neither idea represents how the recipients of the label have viewed it. They have tended to feel instead that they are the victims of a stigma, that they are not good enough to win a place in the starting line-up. David Fairclough himself complained, 'I felt it handicapped me and only really appreciated being remembered for it when I had finished playing.'[106]

Even a player of the calibre of Manchester United's Ole Gunnar Solskjær has felt the need to excise this image. Solskjær has become synonymous with the role of super-sub, yet the description is not borne out by the figures. He has scored ninety-one Premiership goals in 235 appearances for United up to the end of the 2006–2007 season, with sixteen goals coming in his eighty appearances as a substitute. That's roughly one every five games, yet his record of seventy-four in his 148 starts is the equivalent of one every two games.[107] His chance of scoring would seem to depend upon how many minutes he spends on the pitch rather than the timing of his entrance. It's only his exploits as a sub in especially important games, such as his winning goal in the 1999 Champions League Final, and such feats as scoring four times in eleven minutes against Nottingham Forest in the same year that give a contrary impression. A young Ian Wright gained the same reputation at Crystal Palace after he came off the bench to score two goals in a Cup Final against Manchester United, but he had no trouble scoring over the full ninety minutes as an Arsenal player. And even David Fairclough himself once scored a hat-trick when Bob Paisley allowed him to start a game, but he was back on the bench for the next match.

Some players are believed to be better suited to the substitute role because they do not have the fitness to play a full game. For example, Paul Peschisolido acquired a reputation as a 'lower league Ole Gunnar Solskjær' in the latter part of his career at Sheffield United and Derby County. Thirty-five years old in 2007, he does not have the legs to play at full throttle for ninety minutes. However, at the end of February 2007, his statistics were as follows: ninety-five league goals in 270 starts (one every 2.8 games) and ten in 108 appearances as a substitute (one every 10.8 games). Peschisolido has not done appreciably better coming on in the last twenty minutes than when he plays only the first twenty minutes.

The fact is that when they are not limited to short bursts of action for reasons of age or fitness, so-called super-subs tend to be very good players no matter when they make their entrance. Where such strong, rich and famous sides as Manchester United and Liverpool are concerned, it should be no surprise that their substitutes benches contain players of exceptional skill. The Galacticos of Real Madrid kept even Michael Owen on the bench. Despite the criticism Owen received from the Spanish press, he became La Liga's top scorer in goals compared to number of minutes played. He effectively became a super-sub, but no one associates him with the term in

England because he has not been used as a substitute for Liverpool, Newcastle or the England team. Owen left Real because no striker wants to be a substitute, super or otherwise. All footballers strive for a place in the starting line-up. This is not just for the joy of playing for longer or the prestige of being in the club's best eleven, but because more time on the pitch means more chance to shine and more chance to score goals.

How do the dimples on a golf ball work?

The New Zealand cartoonist Burton Silver invented a golf ball shaped like an egg that he claimed was far superior to the ordinary version. The unique shape makes it easier to control, in that it cannot be hooked or sliced because it spins on two axes. It was, however, never likely to sweep the golfing world as it made putting impossible. Silver was not going to be defeated, and he invented 'golfcross', a sport that does away with greens and uses nets instead of holes. This breakaway meant that the most important innovation in golf ball design remains the dimple.

The first golf balls were made from wood. They were superseded by 'featheries', in which a core of compressed goose feathers was stuffed inside a leather shell that was shrunk to fit. The next generation of balls, the 'gutties', were made from the rubbery sap of the gutta tree – which resulted in a perfectly smooth ball but one that failed to fly as far as the old. Thus the properties of dimples were discovered and designers set about bettering the natural perforations and battle scars of the old leather balls. Today's professional balls consist of a plastic shell surrounding a layer of rubber threads and a gel core, though ordinary golfers use a simpler, cheaper two-piece rubber and plastic ball. Most modern balls have between 330 and 500 dimples, with the top players having theirs tailor-made with the optimum number of depressions to suit their swing.

A sphere is not an ideal shape for an object in flight. Because the rear of the ball decreases in diameter to a point over a short distance, the air the ball cuts through is forced to come back together very quickly to fill the vacuum behind it. In the process, the air in the ball's wake breaks up into swirls and eddies that exert less force on its rear than does the more smoothly moving air to the front. As a result, the ball in flight suffers the effects of drag. This is why aeroplanes (and the helmets that speed cyclists and downhill skiers wear) are designed with tapering tails – to allow the air to come back together more slowly without creating swirls and eddies. Dimples intervene by creating a thin layer of turbulence close to the ball's surface that allows the smoothly flowing air to continue its progress around the ball further than it would otherwise manage. This creates a much smaller wake. The effect is so pronounced that a dimpled ball can travel twice as far as the smooth version.

Different kinds of dimples are suitable for different weather conditions. Shallow depressions generate more back-spin than the deeper variety, which means more lift and a ball that stays in the air longer. Wider dimples give a higher trajectory and a longer the time in the air, but allow for less control in the wind.

What are the upper limits of sporting performance?

According to conventional wisdom, improvements in world record times and distances in athletics are levelling off, indicating that we are close to reaching the absolute limits of human performance. The history of the 100 metres world record is the one most cited in support, as undeniably it is being broken by ever smaller increments. As can be seen in the table below, reductions of one hundredth of a second have become the norm:

Donald Lippincott	10.6	06 July 1912
Charles Paddock	10.4	23 April 1921
Percy Williams	10.3	09 August 1930
Jesse Owens	10.2	20 June 1936
Willie Williams	10.1	03 August 1956
Armin Hary	10.0	21 June 1960
Jim Hines	9.95	14 October 1968
Calvin Smith	9.93	03 July 1983
Carl Lewis	9.92	24 September 1988
Leroy Burrell	9.90	14 June 1991
Carl Lewis	9.86	25 August 1991
Leroy Burrell	9.85	06 July 1994
Donovan Bailey	9.84	27 July 1996
Maurice Greene	9.79	16 June 1999
Asafa Powell	9.77	14 June 2005

However, if we look at greater increments, where the world record has improved by one tenth of a second or more (sometimes requiring several smaller improvements along the way), it does not look as though the pace of improvement is slowing down at all:

	Donald Lippincott	10.6
9 years later:	Charles Paddock	10.4
9 years later:	Percy Williams	10.3
6 years later:	Jesse Owens	10.2
20 years later:	Willie Williams	10.1
4 years later:	Armin Hary	10.0
31 years later:	Leroy Burrell	9.90
8 years later:	Maurice Greene	9.79

There is no clear pattern in these intervals between tenth of a second improvements. It is simply not true that the graphs are 'levelling off'. While the increments by which the record is broken are diminishing, the rate at which the fastest time is shortening is not. There is also a simple reason why the increments were once larger: timekeeping was done by hand with an old-fashioned stopwatch that did not allow for precise measurements involving hundredths of a second. If a human limit is soon to be reached in the 100 metres then, we cannot deduce this on the basis of the history of the world record.

It is of course possible that we are looking in the wrong place for our evidence, and that the limit was in fact reached some time ago. Eight men have bettered Carl Lewis's world record of 9.8 set in 1988. However, peak speed – the maximum speed reached over a ten-metre segment – has not increased since Lewis reached 43.47 kph during that race. Even Ben

Johnson could only equal this figure. The improvement has instead been made up largely from faster reactions to the starting pistol. Improvement has an imposed limit here, for since 2002 the rules have stated that a reaction of less than 100 milliseconds is to be counted as a false start. Normal reaction times are between 120 and 160 ms, so breaking the world record might come down to a lucky – but not *too* lucky – anticipation of the gun. It might also come down to the vagaries of measurement, since wind readings are accurate only to within 0.9 m/s, which translates to 0.05 seconds of running time.[108]

In 2006, Pierre-Jean Vazel, a French statistician and sprinting coach, constructed a hypothetical race involving the best runners of all time giving their fastest performances on the fastest surfaces. He adjusted their best race times by putting together their fastest starts, maximum speeds at various stages of a race and the maximum legal tailwind of 2 m/s. According to his results, Justin Gatlin is capable of a time of 9.76 and Asafa Powell of 9.75. But Ben Johnson would be well ahead of the field – smashing the world record in a time of 9.58. This would, of course, incorporate his most intensely drug-fuelled days on the track. Edward Coyle, the director of the Human Performance Laboratory at the University of Texas at Austin, made similar projections for the marathon, based on the human body's ability to utilize oxygen. Paul Tergat ran a world record time of 2:4:55 in 2003, but according to Coyle it should be possible to reduce this to 1:57:48. The difference is so significant that it would be equivalent to all the improvement that has taken place since 1965.

Improvements obviously cannot go on for ever. Although training methods continue to advance, with throwing and jumping actions analysed with video and computer equipment and diets tailored for maximal performance, the chief gains have already been made in the move to professionalism itself. For world-class athletes today, training is a full-time job. By contrast, Roger Bannister's last- minute preparations for the first four-minute mile are rumoured to have included a cigarette in the changing rooms.

Some of the improvements in the past were due to the introduction of starting blocks, running spikes and hi-tech track surfaces. In other events the effect of technology has been even greater. The world record in the pole vault stands 80 per cent higher than in 1896 largely thanks to the aluminium, steel and then fibreglass poles that replaced the original bamboo, while Dick Fosbury's famous flop that enabled high jumping records to be shattered would have led to a broken neck without the invention of synthetic crash mats to replace the traditional sand pit.

Equally significant has been the introduction of new populations to the Olympic and world sporting arena, whether they be African Americans or athletes from developing countries who had never previously had the opportunity to compete. Obviously, the more people jostling for the best times, the more likely it is that records will be broken. The influx of Chinese athletes, with their government's ruthless training programmes for children that recall the excesses of the old Soviet Bloc, has added two billion people to the sporting world's labour pool. It is no wonder that performances are vastly better than when Olympic competition was the preserve of the upper classes. They will go on getting better as the pool continues to increase, with huge untapped reserves in Africa and Asia. Neither is it beyond reasonable doubt that these effects are exceeded by the illicit improvements allowed by performance-enhancing drugs. In this case, a dropping off of record-breaking performances should be expected given the crackdown on drugs in recent years.

If genetic modification fulfils its promise (part of which is to be undetectable by anti-doping measures), then we can expect the upper limits of human performance to match those of the materials of which our bodies are made. Athletes may find their bones snapping if their muscles are strong enough to propel them to the final world record.

Why has Formula One got safer?

In 1999, Mika Hakkinen crashed out of the German Grand Prix at Hockenheim when his McLaren suffered a rear blow-out. The vehicle left the track at 207 mph and slammed into a tyre barrier. Yet one would never guess as much from surveying the 'wreck', which is on display in London's Science Museum. Apart from two flat tyres and a slightly bashed-in nose, the machine looks perfectly serviceable. It is no wonder that Hakkinen was able to walk away from the accident unscathed. What is more surprising is how his good fortune seems to have become so common in Formula One in recent years.

Formula One cars may not have driver airbags, but they do have six seat belts that fasten the driver tightly to his seat (unlike in a road car where they are engineered for a looser fit so that you can root around for maps and adjust the stereo). All six straps can be undone in a single movement and a driver can be out of his car in under five seconds. The steering wheel is designed to be removable to facilitate escape and to be re-attachable for subsequently manoeuvring the car out of the path of others. The driver and the entire seat can easily be lifted out together if necessary.

Drivers wear bespoke crash helmets and fire-retardant body suits. All a driver's soft clothing, including his underpants, are made from Nomex, a synthetic material that can withstand temperatures of 850°C for 35 seconds. Other current safety measures include internal fire extinguishers that discharge into the cockpit and engine, a padded cockpit and, most importantly, the monocoque – the carbon-fibre bathtub that encases the driver in a protective shell twice as strong as solid steel. Even the wheels are tethered so that they cannot go flying into the crowd and injure spectators.

While there were eight deaths in Formula One in the sixties and another eight in the seventies, the toll fell to two in the eighties and two in the nineties, and there have been none since Ayrton Senna died at Tamburello in 1994. Circuit design was rethought following Senna's death, and the FIA identified the twenty-seven most dangerous corners in the world for redevelopment. Larger run-off zones are now being covered with course tarmac instead of gravel to prevent the cars from flipping over.

None of these measures are foolproof – Senna died because his helmet was penetrated, even though the previous year had seen the thickness of drivers' helmets increase. But the driver's wellbeing is no longer the only health concern in the sport. The Science Museum may not have needed to carry out restoration work on Mika Hakkinen's unfortunate McLaren, but they were forced by law to remove one safety hazard that the car had endured during its working lifetime: the tobacco advertising logos.

Can you buy success in football?

Today, only a handful of top sides have even a single first team player who grew up within the same postal district as their stadium. Yet, while it is extremely difficult to achieve success in football without paying for it, history offers a well-stocked graveyard of teams that have paid top dollar for success that never came. Common sense tells us that money has not only to be spent, but spent in the right way. But that hardly counts as advice when the 'right' way to spend money only becomes clear with hindsight. It took the resources of a blue chip city firm to divine the true path to victory.

Between 1996 and 2000, Arsenal spent an average of £5 million a year in the transfer market and achieved an average league position of second. Newcastle, by contrast, spent £11.6 million a year, but only managed to finish seventh on average. Some teams prove to be money pits. For example, Sir Jack Hayward bought Wolverhampton Wanderers in 1990 and proceeded to pour £50 million of his personal fortune into the attempt to return the team to its former glory. In 2003, Wolves were finally promoted to the Premiership after winning the Championship play-offs, but they came straight back down the following season after failing to win a single game away from home. In May 2007, Sir Jack agreed to sell the club for a tenner in return for the promise of a further £30 million investment in the team. Newcastle and Wolves may have suffered from unwise purchases, but the richer clubs often have even more embarrassments to their name. Even the canniest managers have their duds, as Manchester United fans discovered when Alex Ferguson bought Diego Forlan and Juan Sebastian Veron.

The Sports Business Group at Deloitte, the top accountancy and business services firm, however, believe that fans and commentators have been looking at the wrong kind of spending all along. Deloitte has been conducting a yearly analysis of European football with a commentary on the industry since 1992. What emerges is that wage bills represent a far more accurate indicator of performance than transfer fees. The following table for the 2005–6 season is extracted from their *Annual Review of Football Finance 2007*.

	Wages Rank	League Position	Variance	Wage Bill
Chelsea	1	1	0	£114m
Manchester United	2	2	0	£85m
Arsenal	3	4	-1	£83m
Liverpool	4	3	+1	£69m
Newcastle	5	7	-2	£52m
Tottenham Hotspur	6	5	+1	£41m
Aston Villa	7	16	-9	£38m
Everton	8	11	-3	£37m
Manchester City	9	15	-6	£34m
Charlton Athletic	10	13	-3	£34m

Blackburn Rovers	11	6	+5	£33m
West Ham United	12	9	+3	£31m
Fulham	13	12	+1	£30m
Bolton Wanderers	14	8	+6	£29m
Birmingham City	15	18	-3	£27m
Portsmouth	16	17	-1	£25m
Wigan Athletic	17	10	+7	£21m
West Bromwich Albion	18	19	-1	£20m
Sunderland	19	20	-1	£17m

NB: No data was available for Middlesborough.

The table reveals that the performances of various Premiership managers are at odds with their reputations. For example, Alan Curbishley was lauded for keeping Charlton Athletic in the Premiership for so many years, yet given the club's outlay he should have delivered a top ten finish in the 2005–6 season. With a positive variance of seven places, Wigan's Paul Jewell should have narrowly beaten Bolton's Sam Allardyce to the Premiership Manager of the Year Award. In the event, the trophy went, as expected, to Chelsea's free-spending Jose Mourinho. But in Mourinho's defence, it is impossible to generate positive variance if you are the highest spending club.

The Deloitte authors note that there is significantly less correlation between wage costs and final league position in the Championship than in the Premier League. In the Premiership itself, a club's league position is closely correlated with its expenditure on wages. Most of the variance takes place in the middle of the table. Spending extraordinary amounts almost guarantees a high finish while, with the exception of Wigan's startling performance, spending very little by comparison with one's rivals ensures a fight for survival at the end of the season.

How disabled do you have to be to qualify for the Paralympics?

S oon after the Spanish team of mentally disabled basketball players won gold at the Sydney 2000 Paralympics, one of their number revealed himself to be an undercover journalist. Neither Carlos Ribagorda nor nine of his twelve teammates, it transpired, had any sort of disability, mental or physical. He further claimed that five more athletes had cheated their way into other events without passing any physical or psychological tests. The International Paralympic Committee responded by suspending all competitions involving intellectually impaired athletes pending the design of new procedures for preventing similar scandals in the future. But the Athens Games came and went without any reinstatement, and now the innocent majority are set to miss Beijing too. The public reaction was surprise not so much that cheats could slip through the net so easily, but that mere intellectual impairment should be considered a disability when it comes to basketball.

According to the International Paralympic Committee, the 'para-lympics' are so named because they run in 'parallel' to the Olympics. However, the original participants coined the word as a pun on 'paraplegic'. The Games grew out of the sporting events organized to help rehabilitate former servicemen and -women at Britain's National Spinal Injuries Unit at Stoke Mandeville Hospital in 1944. They were named the 'Games for the Paralysed' when the Olympics came to London in 1948, and the competition officially became the Paralympics in Rome in 1960, where 400 wheelchair athletes attended. Events for amputees, the visually impaired and those with cerebral palsy were added later. Today, competitors are divided into fifty levels of disability in five categories: Amputee, Cerebral Palsy, Intellectual Disability, Wheelchair, Vision-Impaired and 'Les Autres', comprising everyone not covered in the other five. The *IPC Athletics Classification Handbook 2006* declares that: 'The minimum impairment levels include references to muscle power, joint range of movement, spinal deformity, amputation level and congenital limb shortening, spasticity and tendon reflex changes, vision and visual fields, and limb length differences. An athlete, who has more than one impairment either of which does not meet the minimum level, may be eligible to compete. The impairments must impact on the athlete's ability to compete fairly in able-bodied competition.' The summer Games consist of nineteen sports, three of which have no equivalent in able-bodied Olympics: goalball (a relative of handball played by blind athletes), boccia (a form of bowls) and murderball (wheelchair rugby).

To the casual viewer, many events can seem unfair on certain competitors, because while some have obvious disabilities such as missing limbs, others can look almost perfectly able-bodied. Contrary to appearances, however, the authorities carefully band the competitors. Until the Barcelona Olympics, athletes were matched according to disability – with, for example, amputees versus amputees. But since 1992, they have been grouped together according to their functional ability rather than their specific disability. There are exceptions where certain team events involve a spectrum of impairments. For example, in seven-a-side football, every team must field at least one player who has difficulty walking, such that 'usually a small shift in the central equilibrium of these athletes leads to the loss of balance', and no more than three who have only 'mild' locomotive afflictions. There is a similar system for basketball, and in the wheelchair variant athletes can compete even if they do not use a chair in everyday life, so long as their disability makes it impossible for them to compete on their feet against able-bodied basketballers.

Some conditions that would be within one's ability to correct, such as obesity, do not make one eligible to compete even though they may impair athletic function even more severely than other disabilities. The visually impaired still compete at the Paralympics separately. There are three classes of visually impaired athletes, but no one is eligible if they have visual acuity over 6/60 (they can make out the top letter of an optician's chart at six metres which someone with normal vision can see from sixty metres away) and/or a visual field of more than 20 degrees. The Paralympic sport of goalball was specially designed for blind athletes. The ball contains bells so that it can be located by sound, and players must throw it into their opponents' goal. Partially sighted players are blindfolded for fairness. Deafness by itself does not qualify one to compete in the Paralympics. There is a separate Deaflympics, for which athletes must have a hearing loss of at least 55 decibels in the better ear.

Intellectual disabilities featured in the Paralympics for the first time in Atlanta in 1996. Only individuals with an IQ below 75 were allowed to compete. This represents 5 per cent of the population, all of whom experience learning difficulties. This can impinge upon their sporting abilities in different ways. For example, according to the father of Allan Stuart, the 400 metres world record holder in the learning difficulties category, 'It took Allan months to grasp that when the gun went, he should start to run, and when he gets past everyone, he thinks the job's done, and stops running.'[109]

Great ability in team sports has never been correlated with high intelligence. If anything, the opposite seems to be true. Over the years, there have been several English footballers whose low IQs did not impair their ability to play effectively in the Premiership, while the handful of PhDs in high-level sport has been limited largely to the rugby field. Learning difficulties, unless they are extremely severe, are not normally something that has to be overcome in order to attain strength and fitness. But tactical understanding and decision-making can be affected. And their inclusion is at least in line with the original therapeutic ethos of the Paralympics.

Why do some female athletes stop menstruating?

In 1972, President Richard Nixon signed a law requiring all American schools to provide equal sporting opportunities for women. By the end of the century, this had resulted in a ten-fold increase in the number of female students participating in sports. However, by the beginning of the nineties, coaches and doctors had begun to notice a worrying trend among the new intake. Some women's menstrual cycles began to stutter or stop entirely as they trained harder. A myth arose at first – predominantly among male coaches – that the absence of periods (amenorrhea) was a sign of peak fitness, but there were also other significant and less ambiguous correlations. The women who stopped menstruating were often suffering from eating disorders; and stress fractures – relatively common in female athletes compared to their male counterparts – were almost three times more common in those with amenorrhea. Together these factors became known as the 'female athlete triad'.

Studies have produced varying estimates of the extent of the problem. Between 15 and 62 per cent of female college athletes in the US exhibit eating disorders, while amenorrhea affects up to 66 per cent, compared with between 2 and 5 per cent of women in the population at large.[110] The picture is worse in sports that require leanness for reasons of efficiency, such as long-distance running, or aesthetics, such as artistic gymnastics and even ballet. A survey carried out by Cleveland State University found that 57 per cent of women's athletics coaches at US universities could not name the elements of the female athletic triad, while a quarter still mistakenly believed that non-existent periods were a natural consequence of intensive exercise rather than the result of an eating disorder.[111]

According to research published in *The Lancet*, exercise has no special disruptive effect on menstrual function.[112] Although female athletes are more likely to suffer amenorrhea than more sedentary individuals, it is not because they are doing athletics. The problem is that some of them are not consuming enough calories to fuel their physical activity. As their bodies starve, the menstrual cycle shuts down and oestrogen levels plummet. Oestrogen is essential for maintaining bone density in women, so it is possible for an athlete in her twenties or even earlier to suffer osteoporosis. The triad is completed when she ends up with the bones of a 60- or 70-year-old. Hence the prevalence of stress fractures.

In very young athletes with a punishing training regime, menstruation may get delayed into their twenties, risking long-term infertility in addition to the other effects of the triad. This was alleged to have been a deliberate policy in the Soviet Union, where the lives of young gymnasts were less important than national glory. The same is alleged of China today, but even in the United States the best gymnasts are training forty hours a week by the time they are 12 years old. However, the same voices that condemn this abuse of women are generally the first to cry sexism when it is suggested that girls should not be permitted to train as hard as boys.

What accounts for home advantage?

In March 2001, the Brazilian football team travelled to humble Ecuador to play a qualifier for the 2002 World Cup. The home side, at that time ranked seventy-fifth in the world by FIFA, managed to pull off a shock 1-0 victory against a team that included Romario and Rivaldo. During the campaign for the 2006 tournament, Ecuador again beat Brazil 1-0 at home, following up with a 2-0 victory over Argentina. In all, they won seven and drew two of their home qualifiers. Yet their away matches were a disaster – comprising six losses, two draws and just one win.

The explanation lies in their nation's geography: Ecuador's home stadium of Atahualpa in Quito sits at 9,200 feet (2,800 metres) above sea level, and opposing teams typically could afford only minimal time for acclimatization. Ecuador's solitary away win was at a similarly high altitude at La Paz in Bolivia. The Peruvian FA had taken note and were considering moving their national stadium from sea-level Lima to Cuzco in the Andes (altitude 10,000 feet) before FIFA international matches above 9,840 feet were outlawed in June 2007.

The reasons for home advantage are rarely so obvious, but the advantage itself is ever present and undeniable even when there are no major mountain ranges involved. In the

English Football League, around 65 per cent of a soccer team's wins are achieved playing at home. According to one study, home advantage is worth an extra 0.44 goals per match.[113] It's telling that part of this advantage is lost when a team relocates to a new ground, as Thierry Henry found when Arsenal moved to the Emirates Stadium. Having played in the team that missed twenty-four chances between them in their goalless draw against CSKA Moscow in November 2006, he explained, 'With my back to goal I still don't know for certain where I am. There are goals I scored at Highbury which I haven't tried at the Emirates Stadium. The visual reference points are different. It's going to take a while playing there for us to find our markers.'[114] If this is true, then stadium designers should incorporate irregular patterns and landmarks into their designs to help home strikers get used to the layout.

The traditional view of home advantage is that the support of a large crowd stiffens players' resolve and inspires them to fight for every ball. Baseball teams with domed stadia have been found to enjoy a stronger home advantage than those with open-air grounds, probably due to the concentration of crowd noise.[115] In baseball, home teams are more likely to win on the opening day of the season than during regular or championship games – an effect accentuated by playing in front of a full house. Teams want to make a good first impression on the fans, who in turn have the pent-up energy of the close season to let out.[116] In 2002, a group of psychologists at Northumbria University led by Sandy Wolfson and Nick Neave tested the saliva of soccer players before home and away fixtures.[117] They found that their testosterone level was unchanged from the male average before away matches and training sessions but rose by 40 per cent an hour before home games. The effect was particularly pronounced among goalkeepers. The researchers linked the findings to the effects of territoriality.

However, home grounds, and home crowds, appear to confer no great advantage in tennis or golf (barring the Ryder Cup match at Brookline in 1999 when Andrew Coltart's ball was surreptitiously stamped into the ground by fans during his game against Tiger Woods). It would seem that this is because refereeing decisions are less subjective in those sports and therefore less open to influence by a partisan crowd. In the Olympic Games, subjectively judged events such as gymnastics and figure skating exhibit a stronger home advantage than those events judged by time, speed and distance.

Repeated studies have shown that away sides garner more red and yellow cards. In the higher leagues where large crowds are the norm, home teams enjoy as much as 70 per cent of the penalties awarded and suffer as few as 30 per cent of the red cards.[118] This may be because abusive crowds goad visiting players into committing more fouls and taking more chances with the hope of 'sticking it up to them'. If aggression is the deciding factor, then it may be that away teams are penalized more often because they spend more time defending during the match. But this cannot be the whole story. In 1999, two groups of footballers, referees and coaches were given video footage to watch of fifty-two challenges in a soccer match and asked to make their own rulings on the offences. One group watched the footage with the sound off. Those who watched the unexpurgated version were significantly influenced by the background noise to favour the home team.[119] Perhaps it is no wonder that Manchester United famously conceded only three penalties in ten years at Old Trafford – all of which were missed.

Could a rugby player make it in the NFL?

Few would guess that the USA are the reigning Olympic rugby champions, having won the title the last time rugby formed part of the Olympic Games in Paris in 1924. Least of all the Americans themselves, though what they call 'football' was adapted from the rugby played in East Coast colleges such as Princeton and Harvard in the late nineteenth century. Aficionados of the English game do not always appreciate just how much it has evolved in the US and how Byzantine and brutal it has become at the highest level. Every few years sees another star of rugby fancy their chances in gridiron. Each time it ends the same way – the press reports meetings with NFL scouts and agents and rumours of multi-million-dollar contracts, then little is heard of their ambition ever again.

Some rugby fans are surprised that their idols would not be tough enough to play in the NFL. After all, they do not wear pads and helmets or get breaks every few minutes like their gridiron counterparts. Whereas rugby is a contact sport, American football is often described as a 'collision' sport. Researchers at Virginia Tech fitted sensors to the helmets of their college team and recorded impacts of up to 130 G (130 times the force of Earth's gravity).[120] Players took around five hits of 120 G to the head per game, and according to project leader Stefan Duma, 'An impact of 120 G would be like a severe car accident which you could survive if you were wearing a seatbelt.'[121]

These were only college players, and the heaviest NFL linemen generate even greater forces during their clashes. In rugby, backs weigh around 200 pounds and forwards around 240 pounds. In the NFL, there are currently over five hundred players weighing more than 300 pounds signed to training camp rosters. 'Offensive tackles' – the players whose job it is to block running plays – weigh in at an average of 318 pounds across the league. Neither are they slow for their size. As for the fastest men in gridiron – the running backs – Michael Bennett of the Kansas City Chiefs has run 40 metres in 4.27 seconds and 100 metres in 9.91 seconds – faster than Carl Lewis's 1988 world record and enough to win gold in the Olympic Games that year. The fastest man in top-class rugby, South Africa's winger Bryan Habana, has managed 'only' 10.4 seconds for the 100 metres and 4.66 seconds for a 40 metre dash. The great All Blacks winger Jonah Lomu was 6'5" tall, weighed 19 stone and could run the 100 metres in 10.8 seconds. For these statistics he was famously described as 'a freak' by England's captain, Will Carling. But in the NFL Lomu would be nothing out of the ordinary. He is sometimes cited as a player who could have made the transition to American football, because he was such an all-round talent. Yet the NFL is not primarily a place for all-rounders. Each position is a highly specialized role.

The most plausible of these roles for a rugby player to switch to is the 'place-kicker' – the player who sits out the game until called upon to convert touchdowns. The most celebrated example would be Mick Luckhurst, born in Redbourn,

Hertfordshire, who became a mainstay of the Atlanta Falcons during the eighties. The ball is smaller and harder in gridiron, but place-kicking would appear to be an easy job for a seasoned fly half, as every shot takes place directly in front of the posts. Luckhurst himself likes to point out that in rugby, the rules allow Jonny Wilkinson a full minute to prepare himself to take a kick, unmolested by opposing players. In converting a touchdown, on the other hand, he would have less than a second after the ball has been set up, with a wall of large men bearing down upon the ball from only six yards away.[122] That said, Johnny Wilkinson is not bad at drop kicks either – as he proved in the 2003 World Cup Final – and no one holds the ball in place for you for those...

There is at least one example of an American football player becoming a top rugby international. Having previously missed the draft as a college player, Dan Lyle, a 6'4", 245-pound tight end, turned down a contract with the Minnesota Vikings to play as Bath's number 8, where he thrilled crowds with behind-the-back and over-the-head basketball passes. The Vikings contract had been worth twice as much money, but came with no guarantee of making the team. At Bath, Lyle won Man of the Match on his debut, made a *Sunday Times* panel's all-star World XV team in 1998 and prior to that was named the Premiership's Newcomer of the Year and was one of the five finalists for Player of the Year. He also once claimed: 'They all say overseas that whenever we take this game seriously, we'll beat everyone, and it's true. If I could get some All-Pros and train them in rugby, we'd go out and kick ass. Hell, I'll take all those guys who were second-team South-Eastern Conference but didn't make the NFL.'[123]

Not everyone agrees. 'I'll tell you what would happen to the Americans,' predicts Gil Thompson, an NFL players' agent. 'They would get beat to death.'[124] Thompson speaks with experience, as he once took twelve young players to Australia at the behest of Bernie Gross, a sports lawyer who sought to revolutionize rugby by bringing in superior athletic talent. Gross had noted that in Australia there is one professional rugby league club for every 500,000 inhabitants, whereas the US has one NFL club per nine million people, meaning that legions of athletes are unemployed. But although his players were bigger, stronger and faster than the Australians, they lacked the instinctive feel for the game that their hosts had honed over many years of practice. Apparently, they had a problem remembering to put the ball down on the ground after running over the try line.

Dan Lyle can imagine bringing men to rugby 'who don't want to work for $25,000 a year at Kmart when they could be full-time athletes making $100,000, playing a sport that's pretty damn fun.' If money is the issue, then it is significant that no established rugby stars have enjoyed Lyle's success in the other direction. The highest paid rugby players are not far off minimum wage for the NFL, where the average salary in 2006 was $1.4 million. If making the transition was a serious prospect, then many rugby players would leap at the chance to earn such rewards. It is telling that so few have tried.

Why do Americans hate football?

Contrary to popular belief, the Americans have never lobbied for 'extra-time multi-ball' as a means of settling the World Cup Final. But the story captures perfectly the boredom and contempt with which the average American regards soccer. Some have long suspected the game to be a communist plot to lure red-blooded Americans away from more manly sports such as baseball and gridiron. Admittedly, Minnesota does boast an official Commie Soccer League, but Baltimore's pinko-sounding CCCP FC stands for 'Charm City Cunt Punchers'. In the US, sport is something you do with your hands, and the only self-respecting American males seen kicking a ball are under twelve. There are rather a lot of the latter. Soccer is played by around eighteen million schoolchildren, even if half of them are girls. It is particularly popular among less athletic students because, as the American novelist Dave Eggers puts it, 'There is no other sport that can bear such incompetence. With soccer, twenty-two kids can be running around, most of them aimlessly, or picking weeds by the sidelines, or crying for no apparent reason, and yet the game can have the general appearance of an actual soccer match.'[125] All this comes to an end for the vast majority as they enter their teens.

Americans themselves offer various reasons for their distaste, not all of which can be true. One is that they are so insular that they cannot stand sports they are no good at. While uncharacteristically self-critical, this is not quite accurate. There are plenty of underachieving but well-supported sports teams in the USA. The Boston Red Sox had no shortage of devoted fans through the long decades they went without a World Series win. Before the USA World Cup in 1994, there was an absurd level of optimism about the home team's chances, but this optimism was not born of any enthusiasm. In any case, American teams do not fare particularly well against international opposition in basketball or baseball either, yet this does not harm their popularity. Perhaps Americans are more tolerant when sports they invented are concerned. However, they did not create golf, and five Ryder Cup defeats in six years have not dulled their appetite for that. The victory of Team USA in the women's soccer World Cup in 1991 and 1999 shows that the low achievement of their menfolk is more likely a consequence rather than a cause of the lack of interest in the sport.

Americans also complain that soccer is simply not engaging as a spectacle. Soccer is 'too slow', with long periods of aimless passing and far too much build-up. Even if this charge was defensible, they seem to love the much slower game of golf, which boasts huge television audiences. Baseball too is not the fastest of games. Besides, they would supposedly like to slow soccer down further by inserting four advertising breaks. Closely allied is another gripe: there aren't enough goals. Many soccer fans would agree with them. Americans may lack the patience to appreciate the gradual dismantling of a defence, but then so do many of the rest of us. It was FIFA officials, not American sponsors, who first suggested widening the goals and prohibiting defensive walls at free kicks, while the recent idea of reducing teams to ten men in order to create more space for attacking players came from the Brazilians. On average, only 2.29 goals were scored per match in the 2006 World Cup – almost as few as the all-time low of 2.21 during Italia '90.

However, the paucity of goals is one of the things that makes soccer worth watching, because it means that no result is ever a foregone conclusion. The lower the scoreline, the greater the chance of an upset. Lower league clubs occasionally defeat Premiership outfits in FA Cup ties, but the scoreline is almost always 1-0 or 2-1, never 5-4. Better teams score more goals than weaker ones over a period of time, so the more goals that are scored in a match, the greater chance that the majority will come from the stronger side. If Manchester United score five times as many goals as Lincoln City in the long run, then the League Two minnows can expect to win once in every six encounters between the two teams where only a single goal is scored, or 17 per cent of the time. In matches that feature three goals, they can expect to win just once in fourteen games, or 7 per cent of the time. In nine-goal bonanzas, poor Lincoln would win less than 1 per cent of the time. Low-scoring games also mean that the result more often remains in doubt right up to the end. A soccer team can snatch a draw with a single goal in the dying seconds, but if a basketball team is 40 points down with five minutes to run then the spectators might as well go home.

In ice hockey, Colorado Avalanche's 1-0 win over the Florida Panthers in the final game of the 1996 Stanley Cup is considered a classic – principally because the Colorado keeper was called upon to make sixty-three saves. It's action that the American sports fan craves, not goals per se. Cricket is a high-scoring game and Americans have no time for that. Moreover,

Test matches often end in a draw, which Americans hate even more than a low-scoring game. Draws are forbidden in baseball and basketball, while they have been rendered extremely rare in the NFL. Americans have changed the rules of their home-grown sports many times over the past century to please sports fans, but they lack the authority to tamper with soccer. Italia '90's goal famine prompted FIFA to eliminate back passes to the goalkeeper and introduce three points for a win in the group stage. These tiny changes were historic for such a slow-moving organization, but similar tinkering has been the norm in American sports. Basketball is far more popular in its present high-scoring incarnation than in previous decades when travelling and palming were more heavily penalized.

Major League Soccer has lost more than $350 million since its inception in 1993, but several teams are already covering their costs and the operation looks to have more longevity than the defunct North American Soccer League that once tempted Pelé and George Best to the United States. But if David Beckham thinks he is going to convert the locals to the beautiful game, one look at MLS's fan base should disabuse him. He has been brought to California not to tempt spectators away from baseball and basketball, but largely to entertain the Spanish-speaking migrants who fill the land's soccer stadia. Hispanic Americans make up over a third of the crowds. For most Americans, sport is already a saturated market, with the NFL, baseball, basketball and ice hockey making demands on the fans' attention. But new spectacles can still make an impact. For example, Ultimate Fighting now garners more pay-per-view revenue than boxing.

It is no coincidence that the latest sport to make it big in the States involves an excess of machismo. In this it could not be more different to the American perception of soccer. The game's irretrievable image problem begins at high school, where it is the sport of choice for those not tough enough for gridiron. This conclusion is reinforced whenever soccer appears on television, where grown men throw themselves to the ground, feigning injury at the slightest contact. Violent conduct is more or less permitted in the NFL, but there is zero tolerance of faking. An individual like Cristiano Ronaldo would not be accepted in American sport, let alone showered with Player of the Year awards. All American sportsmen are described as 'athletes' – even if their game is basketball or hockey – and that reflects what they think a professional sportsman should be. Americans sometimes confess that, to their ears, all Englishmen sound gay. It appears that Vinnie Jones and Norman Hunter are no exceptions.

Could performance-enhancing drugs turn an ordinary mortal into a top athlete?

When Mark McGwire broke Roger Maris's home-run record in 1998, his 70 homers did almost as much for sales of the muscle-building compound creatine as for baseball attendances. McGwire began to take creatine and androstenedione in 1994 as he recovered from persistent back and neck injuries. Although androstenedione, a testosterone booster, is banned in Olympic competition, there were no restrictions on its use in baseball. Also legal, creatine was extremely popular in the sport in the nineties and was used by several members of the British athletics team, including Olympic gold medallists Linford Christie and Sally Gunnell. Though its results are regarded as extremely mild compared with those that can be achieved with steroids, so are its side effects: instead of withering your testicles and making you grow breasts, you're likely only to suffer the odd muscle strain and bout of diarrhoea.

McGwire was a noted power-hitter long before he started taking dietary supplements. He hit 49 home runs in his first season with the Oakland Athletics in 1987 – the highest ever total for a rookie – and made over 50 in each of the three seasons prior to his record-breaking run. But a section of baseball fans will never acknowledge McGwire's place in history. They believe that his achievement will always be tainted by his training methods. Presumably they were pleased when the record was broken once more – by Barry Bonds in 2001. At least until federal prosecutors raised allegations that Bonds had abused steroids, human growth hormone, Depo-Testosterone, insulin and Clomid.

McGwire's home run record was an inspiration to thousands of young players, who left the stadium and went straight to the drug store. Creatine was already available in capsule and powdered form as an over-the-counter dietary supplement, but health food shops also posted a brisk trade in foul-tasting creatine-laced chocolate bars. It enables an athlete to exercise harder and improves the recovery time after an intense bout, which helps in 'power' sports, though not in endurance events. At the turn of the millennium, 28 per cent of college athletes in the US were reportedly taking creatine.[126] Of the eight teams involved in the College World Series competition in McGwire's record year, every one included athletes who used creatine in their training. Estimates of the substance's efficacy vary, but it is thought to offer up to 20 per cent of the results that can be attained with illegal steroids. This would certainly not be enough to turn a couch potato into a decent sprinter or weightlifter, but it could give a top competitor an appreciable edge in the 100 metres, where races are won by extremely narrow margins.

Steroid abusers can take up to a hundred times the doses legally prescribed by doctors. The medical profession is agreed on the general effects of steroids and most other performance-enhancing drugs, but for ethical reasons there have been no significant experiments conducted to determine the effects of large doses upon athletic ability. However, there have been several small-scale trials, and one can estimate the consequences of drug use by an ordinary Joe by looking at the performances achieved by certain athletes before and after they began using drugs. A German study of fifteen weightlifters in the seventies recorded a 7 per cent increase in performance after a three-month course of nandrolone.[127] In 2004, eighteen amateur male athletes in Australia given weekly injections of testosterone reported a 10 per cent increase in cycling performance and bench-pressing ability above that of a control group after a six-week exercise regimen.[128] These results are so significant that if they were replicated in the world at large, a 'clean' weightlifter would stand little chance of success in his sport if even a handful of top competitors were using drugs. Yet according to David Cowan of the Drug Control Centre at King's College London, the speed of the effects and the infrequency of testing mean that 'in the random testing scenario, it could conceivably make it more likely you could slip through without being tested... We may be catching 10 per cent of those using the drug.'[129]

The British sprinter Dwain Chambers reportedly began taking the steroid THG in spring 2002. He had broken the juniors' 100 metres world record in 1997 with a time of 10.06 seconds, but he did not fulfil his potential and 9.97 was to be the best he could manage without chemical assistance. In September 2002, however, he equalled the European record of 9.87 seconds. Chambers told BBC Sport, 'I don't believe THG had anything to do with the fact that I ran 9.87 seconds. That came about because I was in a world record race and was dragged along.'[130] Others would say that a banned substance had knocked a tenth of a second off his personal best – a considerable result in the 100 metres...

The disgraced US runner Tim Montgomery enjoyed even better results while they lasted. He clocked a 'clean' 9.92 seconds in the 100 metres in 1997, but his best days looked to be behind him when he failed to qualify for the 2000 Olympics in Sydney. That year he failed to run under 10.1 seconds (after adjusting for wind assistance). Yet the following year he ran 9.87 and then in 2002 broke Maurice Greene's world record with a time of 9.84 seconds. He subsequently admitted to taking steroids and human growth hormone supplied by the now notorious BALCO laboratory, and his records from 31 March 2001 onwards were expunged. Drugs seem to have helped Montgomery improve by up to 0.14 seconds.

In highly competitive sports where very little separates the top athletes, these effects can make the difference between an Olympic gold medal and failure to qualify for the final. But hundredths or tenths of a second would be far from enough to turn an ordinary mortal into a world-beater. Trevor 'the Tortoise' Misapeka, a 22-stone American Samoan, ran a 100 metres heat in 14.28 seconds at the 2001 World Championships – four seconds slower than the winner. To get close to the sprint specialists through drugs alone he would have to take so many steroids that he would find himself competing as a member of the opposite sex before he made any impression at a track meet.

Why are there so few Asian footballers in Britain?

'Their ankles are weak'; 'they don't eat the right food'; 'they only play cricket' – these are just some of the excuses offered by coaches and scouts for why we see so few Asian footballers. In another era, the same men would have dismissed Afro-Caribbean players as 'lacking stamina' and 'no good in cold weather', yet black players now make up over a quarter of the Premiership's personnel. In 1996, Jas Bains and Raj Patel produced a report titled 'Asians Can't Play Football' – an attitude they found to be endemic in the sport's administration. Sixty-nine per cent of club officials believed that Asians lacked the physique to play professionally, while many thought that they were simply not interested in soccer. This was five years after researchers at Manchester University found that football was even more popular among Bengalis than whites. As for any supposed differences in build, football is unique among contact sports in welcoming the gamut of healthy body shapes – as can be seen from an England forward line that teams Peter Crouch (6'7") with Michael Owen (5'8"). More than a decade after Bains and Patel's report, very little has changed.

The answer is racism, but not the kind we might have assumed. We ought not to forget from the outset that fewer and fewer home-grown players of any race, white or black, are making it into Premiership sides. Englishmen represent only 40 per cent of current top-flight players. Asians make up around 3.5 per cent of the English population, which means that out of the five hundred or so regular players in the Premiership, we should expect to see only seven Asian faces. However, even this modest tally is seven more than we saw after the departure of Michael Chopra from Newcastle and Zesh Rehman from Fulham. In August 2006 there were only three Asian professionals in the entire English football league.

Sir Herman Ouseley, head of the 'Kick Racism Out of Football' campaign, alleges that discrimination is at work. Certainly, there is a dearth of ethnic minorities among the senior administration of most clubs and it would be naive to think that all scouts and coaches are free from racist attitudes. However, Zesh Rehman, the first Asian in the Premiership, has denied ever having experienced racism at the professional level. Sport is a meritocracy. With so much money at stake in the modern game, clubs cannot afford to be so unprofessional as to bar players based on the colour of their skin. They would also like to attract Asian fans, who at present only thinly populate the crowds at stadia in the heart of their communities. Clubs such as West Ham and Bradford have accordingly made extensive efforts to engage their local Asian populations. Rehman's own view is that 'The main reason that a lot of British Pakistanis don't make it as footballers is because they don't get enough support off their parents. A lot of our culture revolves around education and I think a lot of parents are wary of their children getting too involved in sport.'[131] In so far as this attitude exists among Asian families, it is more likely to change now that sports stars earn many times the salaries of doctors and lawyers.

Huddersfield Town's Adnan Ahmed cites a form of self-segregation whereby young Asians are often to be seen kicking a ball around with each other but are less likely to get involved in Sunday leagues where they might be spotted by scouts. As Stockport's Harpal Singh put it, 'The problem for most Asian kids is that they have been brought up to play for their own teams in their own leagues and when they are offered a trial at a professional club, they're stepping into the unknown. They are taken away from where they feel comfortable and have to train with lads they've never met before. Understandably they find it difficult to show what they can do.'[132] In the twenty-first century, all-Asian local leagues are still a feature of football up and down the country, whereas the establishment of whites-only leagues would provoke civil disorder. Which begs the question why enthusiastic Asian players feel the need to segregate their teams. The obvious answer is that the anti-racist ethos of the FA has yet to filter down to the local league level, where 65 per cent of Asians say that they have suffered racial abuse during matches.[133]

How inbred are thoroughbred racehorses?

Since 1793, the lineage of every pedigree thoroughbred foal has been recorded in the *General Stud Book*. The first edition detailed some eighty horses brought to England from the Middle East and North Africa in the seventeenth and eighteenth centuries. In 2005, Patrick Cunningham, Trinity College Dublin's Professor of Animal Genetics, trawled the records and used DNA analysis of living horses to demonstrate that most of their bloodlines eventually dwindled. The 500,000 thoroughbred horses in the world today are all descended from twenty-five mares and just three stallions – the Darley Arabian, the Byerley Turk and the Godolphin Barb. Brought to England in 1704 by Thomas Darley, the British consul in Syria, the Darley Arabian alone is responsible for the Y chromosome of 95 per cent of stallions today.

Inbreeding is becoming even more of an issue now that a stallion put out to stud can cover more than two hundred mares each season. Professor Cunningham found that the proportion of genes shared by any two thoroughbreds had risen to 47 per cent, compared with 31 per cent two hundred years ago. All this makes one wonder how severely inbred animals can represent the peak of physical perfection for their species when a similar lineage would guarantee profound disability in humans. In fact, the effects are not harmless for horses either. The thoroughbreds in the starting boxes win their places after a process of attrition that sees two thirds of their siblings end up as glue or pet food (or sometimes pets) before they ever get near a racecourse. In 2006, Cambridge University's Equine Fertility Unit tracked the progress of 1,022 thoroughbreds born in Newmarket in 1999. Only 347 (34 per cent) had ever been entered for a race.

Those animals that do make it typically run only half as many races as their forebears of thirty years ago. A horse's speed is more important to a breeder than what they call its 'soundness' – its robustness or general constitution. One study by the Royal Veterinary College at the University of London has shown a strong correlation between genes found in many thoroughbred horses and an increased risk of limb fractures. However, this far from confirms the wildest allegations of the animal rights lobby that selective breeding results in widespread birth defects. The great majority of thoroughbreds are born healthy, and if they are more likely to find themselves on a Frenchman's dinner table than in a winners' enclosure this is only because in sport there must be more losers than champions.

Are fascists better at sport?

After the Soviet Union launched the Sputnik1 satellite in 1957, many observers drew the conclusion that communism was better suited than capitalism to fostering scientific progress. But the technology that made the first space mission possible had been developed by German scientists captured during the Second World War. All the Reds had done was put them to work and then claim the credit in the name of Marxism–Leninism. This seemed to be an exception that proved the rule – the result was still 1-0 to totalitarianism, albeit Nazi rather than the communist variety. But ultimately it was the free world that outstripped its rivals in scientific innovation. Even during the war itself, radar, sonar and nuclear weapons were all invented by the Western Allies, and the Axis codes were cracked by the world's first computers operating out of Bletchley Park, England. Other excuses for fascism and communism have proved similarly overblown. For example, in the fifties it was feared that the expanding Soviet economy would soon dwarf that of the free world. Only later was it learned that the Kremlin had simply fabricated its economic indicators. But despite the efforts of Jesse Owens at the 1936 Berlin Olympics, there is one area where the superiority of extreme right-wing political systems still seems to be grudgingly acknowledged: the sporting arena.

Fascist propaganda in the thirties and forties was replete with images of healthy bodies and rippling muscles, while the Soviets favoured muscular men and stout women toiling in factories and fields. When every citizen was a potential soldier, it made sense to inculcate physical prowess from an early age. The performance of the state's representatives in sporting events also reflected glory back upon the nation and its leader. Contrary to popular belief, it is a myth that Benito Mussolini ever made Italy's trains run on time – but his nation did win two football World Cups during his period of office.

More often than not, dictators have been driven to apoplexy in the search for trophies. Adolf Hitler's team managed a creditable third place in the 1934 World Cup, but he had been in power for barely a year. In the 1938 tournament, by which time the Führer had had sufficient time to transform the country in his own image, the national side was knocked out by Switzerland in the first round. Even the Italians, fresh from their World Cup victory in 1934, were defeated in what the English called the 'real' final. Mussolini promised each player a brand new Alfa Romeo and a cash bonus if they beat England in an exhibition match at Arsenal's ground. At what became known as the 'Battle of Highbury' they inflicted broken noses, arms and ankles on their opponents, but the English still won 3-2.

Other right-wing dictators would have scoffed at Mussolini's offer of a shiny convertible. They preferred to use terror tactics to motivate players. Iraq's soccer team had a particularly fraught time under the quasi-fascist Baath Party. Saddam Hussein's feared son Uday instigated a regime of beatings for the national side when he was made head of the

Iraqi Football Federation. He liked to telephone his team at half-time and threaten to cut their legs off and feed them to a pack of dogs. When their fortunes continued to decline under his leadership, he had them beaten on the soles of their feet. Such treatment did nothing to improve their skills, and Iraq duly failed to qualify for the 1994 World Cup Finals. The tactical genius then hit on the idea of making the team kick a concrete football. Uday's presidency of his country's Olympic Committee was no more enlightened. He pocketed his athletes' appearance fees and imprisoned, tortured and executed dozens of them.

Antonio Salazar's Portugal team only qualified for a single soccer World Cup. Even then they were cheating, by fascist standards, in that their star player, Eusebio, was black. It was Salazar's death and the transition to democracy that led to the gradual emergence of the country as a force in world football. With the great Alfredo Di Stefano in Franco's Spanish team, that nation beat Poland 7-2 on aggregate in the first European Championship in 1960, but they were effectively expelled from the tournament for refusing to travel to the Soviet Union on principle. Four years later the two teams met in the final at Madrid's Bernabeu Stadium, where the home side won 2-1. Spaniards often blame Franco for the underachievement of their national side, partly by exacerbating divisions between the Catalan and Basque minorities and the rest of Spain. Real Madrid was a symbol of the dictatorship, at least according to Barcelona fans, and Franco's favoured side won fourteen league titles under his rule. But the influence he allegedly wielded on match officials did not stop Barca winning the Supreme General's Cup (now the Copa del Rey, or 'King's Cup') nine times compared to their rivals' six. Neither could Franco have used underhand methods to bring the European Cup to Real five years in a row between 1956 and 1960.

Fascism and football clearly do not mix but, Uday Hussein notwithstanding, athletics offers a different story. Jesse Owens' achievements were not enough to prevent Hitler's Germany finishing head of the medals table by a comfortable margin at the 1936 Olympics. The Third Reich won thirty-three gold medals, beating the democratic USA with twenty-four. Great Britain could manage only four gold medals. Helping to beat Britain into tenth place were imperial Japan in eighth place with six golds and Mussolini's Italy in fourth with eight. It was a shame that the Reich did not also triumph in the wrestling, for the fourth-placed German communist Werner Seelenbinder had planned to flip Hitler the finger from the winner's podium instead of delivering the Nazi salute. So does all this mean that while fascist dogma sits uncomfortably with games of skill, it can nevertheless inspire its people in the more brutish exertion of power, strength and speed?

Fascist countries were certainly among the first to invest in sporting academies. Athletes benefit from sponsorship, and the state is a wealthy and powerful sponsor. But it is equally likely that the Nazis succeeded because they were ruthless and shameless enough to cast aside the principles of fair competition. In 1935, German doctors developed injectable synthetic testosterone for military use. There is no proof that their invention was used to help the nation's athletes the following year, but it was difficult to question the research team as several of its members ended up in the Soviet Union at the end of the Second World War. There they were put to work in

the sports science programme, where they helped the Soviet and
East German teams cheat their way to success.

Do rugby players really abide by the rules more than other sportsmen?

'**R**ugby is a beastly game played by gentlemen' goes the old saw, whereas 'soccer is a gentleman's game played by beasts'. For some traditionalists, that explains the perceived difference between the conduct of professional rugby players and their counterparts with the round ball. Rugby is played and watched by the middle and upper classes – men who 'know how to behave'. They respect the referee because, unlike soccer stars, they are not spoilt, uncouth, overpaid prima donnas (or morons) given licence by a celebrity culture to trample sportsmanship into the turf. This is of course nonsense, and not only because rugby lacks these class associations outside England. Even in the north of the country, rugby league is a working man's game. But it is also outrageous to suggest that rugby players are any kind of saints on the field in either hemisphere.

Violent conduct is widely regarded as part of the game. Reflecting on the number of times he had been punched in the face during rucks, Scotland's Scott Murray remarked: 'I just like to try and play clever. If you can tug someone back and stop them making a tackle, it helps. I get it week in, week out, so there's no reason why I shouldn't cheat a little bit. Everyone cheats; it's just trying to do it without getting caught.' After his nose was broken by England's Richard Hill at Murrayfield in

2000, he explained: 'He stood on me a few times, and I stood on him, and he elbowed me. Nothing you wouldn't expect in an international.'[134] Rugby players do not even require the heat of a competitive match to provoke a melee. Leicester Tigers and England lock Ben Kay has estimated that a serious punch-up occurs on the Tigers' training ground at least once a month.[135] By this reckoning, the reason that rugby players, unlike footballers, never fake injury is that they would not last five minutes among their own teammates if they showed such weakness. In the soccer world, training ground 'incidents' usually result in one of the parties swiftly leaving the club. Acceptable violence does have its limits, however. In March 2001, John Hopoate of Australia's Wests Tigers league side was found guilty of shoving his fingers up three North Queensland players' anuses during a game. He claimed before a judiciary panel that he had merely been administering 'wedgies' to his opponents, to which one of his victims replied, 'I think I know the difference between a wedgie and a finger up my arse... It's a tough game, but there's no room for that.'[136]

Other forms of gamesmanship are also regarded as more or less normal. For example, Leicester won the Heineken Cup in 2002 after Neil Back took the calculated risk to knock away a Munster put-in in the last minute of the game and deny them a last-gasp opportunity to score a try. The ploy worked and the referee missed the infringement. Back subsequently explained to BBC Sport: 'This game is all about little edges – particularly in finals – and doing what you can to win. That was a very crucial scrum, and I did what I had to do to ensure a win for Leicester. I am not a cheat and I would be very upset if anyone accused me of being one. What I did was part of the professional game. I am sure that other back-row players have done it in the past.'[137] Some attempts to bend the rules can even be lauded. Former England captain Lawrence Dallaglio has been praised for his bravery in throwing himself at the boots of opposition forwards in the hope that they will kick him and give away a penalty.

The All Blacks have developed new tactics for after an opponent has been tackled in order to prevent his team from getting the ball back into play quickly. They frustrate attacks by hanging on to the tackled player and throwing another man into the ruck at speed rather than releasing the opponent as the rules dictate. Yet condemnation of the strategy has been far from universal. Most criticism has come from Australia and South Africa, with the latter accusing rugby's authorities of hypocrisy. As the Springbok captain Johann Muller said of his opposite number, 'If Richie McCaw had blond hair and wore a green jersey or had dreadlocks and wore a gold jersey, he would never finish a Test match.'[138] But others have been more sanguine. For example, Sonny Parker, the Welsh centre, denies that the All Blacks' tactics even amount to cheating: 'They are just streetwise. They move bodies really well and they are very physically strong. It's excellent what they do and it sucks playing against it.'[139] If nothing else, this attitude indicates that the worst offence of all is to get caught. The chief reason that hackles have been raised more than usual over this issue is that the perpetrators have been caught and yet little has been done about it. The cheating itself, if that is what it is, is only to be expected.

No matter how angry players get, there is one recourse they almost never take that is sadly a common sight on soccer pitches: mobbing the referee. That kind of thing takes place in the media instead. In one instance it was alleged that Australian loose head prop Bill Young had his international career curtailed by the Springbok coach Jake White's persistent accusations of illegal plays at scrum time.[140] Referees were incited to pay extra attention to Young such that he suffered for the slightest infringement. Whatever the merits of the individual case, Paddy O'Brien, the International Rugby Board's refereeing co-ordinator, has complained of the way that coaches use the press to undermine officials and insists: 'I think some coaches believe they can use the media to get the upper hand. I am determined that the World Cup will be won by the best team on the paddock, not in newspaper columns and certainly not by a coach running to a newspaper, bleating.'[141]

However, for the most part, during a game at least, a rugby referee's decisions are respected by both sides for a number of reasons. One is that captains are allowed to talk to the referee and ask him to explain his decisions. This helps to defuse difficult situations, especially when the match official can call on video replays in real time to inform his judgement. There is also the extra sanction of the sin bin where players can be sent to cool off, and the option of forcing dissenters to move back ten metres – a potentially crucial distance during a match. There is also the nature of rugby as a higher scoring game than soccer to consider. When so many soccer matches are settled by a single goal it is bound to be tempting for players to try to goad or con the referee into awarding a penalty. With far more scoring taking place in rugby, each decision is less significant.

Which nation is the best at sport?

The citizens of the United States believe their nation to be the finest in the world. In the performance of their economy, the output of their artists and scientists, the might of their military and the extent of their charity they are unrivalled. But they also believe themselves to be the world's superpower when it comes to sport. At first sight, the evidence appears to bear them out. To the great frustration of countries that guzzle fewer hamburgers, the USA fares very well in the Olympic Games, which are probably the best all-round test of a nation's sporting prowess. However, a closer inspection of their results reveals that the superpower is a paper tiger on the sporting field.

The final standings at the 2004 Athens Olympic Games were as follows:

Nation		Gold	Silver	Bronze	Total
1	United States	36	39	27	102
2	China	32	17	14	63
3	Russia	27	27	38	92
4	Australia	17	16	16	49
5	Japan	16	9	12	37
6	Germany	13	16	20	49
7	France	11	9	13	33

8	Italy	10	11	11	32
9	South Korea	9	12	9	30
10	Great Britain	9	9	12	30

NB: The official rankings are ordered according to gold medals rather than overall podium finishes.

As in most summer Olympic contests, the world's biggest economies dominated the top ten. But Australia's position should be unexpected, for although the nation boasts a strong economy, its population is far smaller than that of its rivals in the list. China won twice as many gold medals as Australia, but needed a population sixty-five times larger to do so. Australia seems to be punching far above its weight for a country with only the thirty-fourth largest population in the table. Further up the list, it is no surprise to find that the top two positions are taken by the world's largest economy and its most populous nation. Financial investment has a significant bearing on sporting success, but so does a large pool from which to draw athletes.

If we adjust for population size, the medals table looks very different. In terms of gold medals per million citizens, the USA now drops to thirty-third place, only one spot higher than the Dominican Republic, beaten by such sporting powerhouses as Switzerland, Chile and Azerbaijan. China sinks all the way to an ignominious fifty-third, well below Thailand, Uzbekistan and even Kazakhstan. Most embarrassingly of all for the People's Republic, the wayward province of Taiwan ('Chinese Taipei' in the politically correct parlance of international sporting competition) is more than three times as fruitful in gold medals. At least this is better than India, which comes in at sixty-six courtesy of a solitary silver medal, despite having the world's second largest population.

In the following chart adjusted for population, each nation's ranking in the official table is given in parentheses:

Nation			Gold	Silver	Bronze	Total	Population* (in millions)	Golds per million
1	(52)	Bahamas	1	0	1	2	0.30	3.337
2	(17)	Norway	5	0	1	6	4.57	1.093
3	(54)	United Arab Emirates	1	0	0	1	0.92	1.090
4	(4)	Australia	17	16	16	49	19.91	0.854
5	(13)	Hungary	8	6	3	17	10.03	0.797
6	(11)	Cuba	9	7	11	27	11.31	0.796
7	(24)	New Zealand	3	2	0	5	3.99	0.751
8	(34)	Jamaica	2	1	2	5	2.71	0.737
9	(15)	Greece	6	6	4	16	10.65	0.564
10	(19)	Sweden	4	2	1	7	8.99	0.445
11	(32)	Georgia	2	2	0	4	4.69	0.426
12	(37)	Denmark	2	0	6	8	5.41	0.369
13	(29)	Slovakia	2	2	2	6	5.42	0.369
14	(14)	Romania	8	5	6	19	22.36	0.358
15	(45)	Lithuania	1	2	0	3	3.61	0.277
16	(33)	Bulgaria	2	1	9	12	7.52	0.266
17	(18)	Netherlands	4	9	9	22	16.32	0.245
18	(27)	Austria	2	4	1	7	8.17	0.245
19	(44)	Croatia	1	2	2	5	4.50	0.222
20	(26)	Belarus	2	6	7	15	10.31	0.194
21	(12)	Ukraine	9	5	9	23	47.73	0.189
22	(3)	Russia	27	27	38	92	143.78	0.188
23	(9)	South Korea	9	12	9	30	48.60	0.185

24	(7)	France	11	9	13	33	60.42	0.182
25	(8)	Italy	10	11	11	32	58.06	0.172
26	(53)	Israel	1	0	1	2	6.20	0.161
27	(6)	Germany	13	16	20	49	82.42	0.158
28	(10)	Great Britain	9	9	12	30	60.27	0.149
29	(46)	Switzerland	1	1	3	5	7.45	0.134
30	(50)	Azerbaijan	1	0	4	5	7.87	0.127
31	(39)	Chile	2	0	1	3	15.82	0.126
32	(5)	Japan	16	9	12	37	127.33	0.126
33	(1)	United States	36	39	27	102	293.03	0.123
34	(54)	Dominican Republic	1	0	0	1	8.83	0.113
35	(42)	Czech Republic	1	3	4	8	10.25	0.098
36	(51)	Belgium	1	0	2	3	10.35	0.097
37	(21)	Canada	3	6	3	12	32.51	0.092
38	(31)	Chinese Taipei	2	2	1	5	22.75	0.088
39	(49)	Zimbabwe	1	1	1	3	12.67	0.079
40	(23)	Poland	3	2	5	10	38.63	0.078
41	(34)	Uzbekistan	2	1	2	5	26.41	0.076
42	(20)	Spain	3	11	5	19	40.28	0.074
43	(40)	Kazakhstan	1	4	3	8	15.14	0.066
44	(54)	Cameroon	1	0	0	1	16.06	0.062
45	(36)	Morocco	2	1	0	3	32.21	0.062
46	(38)	Argentina	2	0	4	6	39.14	0.051
47	(25)	Thailand	3	1	4	8	64.87	0.046
48	(22)	Turkey	3	3	4	10	68.89	0.044
49	(41)	Kenya	1	4	2	7	32.02	0.031
50	(28)	Ethiopia	2	3	2	7	67.85	0.029
51	(29)	Iran	2	2	2	6	69.02	0.029
52	(16)	Brazil	5	2	3	10	184.10	0.027
53	(2)	China	32	17	14	63	1298.85	0.025

54	(43)	South Africa	1	3	2	6	42.72	0.023
55	(46)	Egypt	1	1	3	5	76.12	0.013
56	(48)	Indonesia	1	1	2	4	238.45	0.004
57	(57)	North Korea	0	4	1	5	22.70	0
58	(58)	Latvia	0	4	0	4	2.31	0
59	(59)	Mexico	0	3	1	4	104.96	0
60	(60)	Portugal	0	2	1	3	10.52	0
61	(61)	Finland	0	2	0	2	5.21	0
62	(61)	Serbia & Montenegro	0	2	0	2	10.83	0
63	(63)	Slovenia	0	1	3	4	2.01	0
64	(64)	Estonia	0	1	2	3	1.34	0
65	(65)	Hong Kong	0	1	0	1	6.86	0
66	(65)	India	0	1	0	1	1065.07	0
67	(65)	Paraguay	0	1	0	1	6.19	0
68	(68)	Colombia	0	0	2	2	42.31	0
69	(68)	Nigeria	0	0	2	2	137.25	0
70	(68)	Venezuela	0	0	2	2	25.02	0
71	(71)	Eritrea	0	0	1	1	4.45	0
72	(71)	Mongolia	0	0	1	1	2.75	0
73	(71)	Syria	0	0	1	1	18.02	0
74	(71)	Trinidad & Tobago	0	0	1	1	1.10	0

* Source: CIA World Factbook 2004.

Some of the standings are deceptive. The world contains many small countries, and the freak success of just one of their athletes in a given year can skew the table away from a faithful representation of various nations' respective prowess. For example, the first and fourth placed nations, the Bahamas and the United Arab Emirates, recorded their first ever gold medals at the 2004 Games. Certain other countries excel in a single type of discipline. Hence Norway tends to do well in comparisons because of its strength in boating events, which have accounted for seven of the country's thirteen gold medals in the last four summer Games. However, in 2004 Australia won gold in events as disparate as cycling, swimming, diving, hockey, rowing and shooting. It should also be pointed out that the Australians won a silver medal in baseball, whereas the United States' baseball team failed to even qualify for the Olympics after losing to Mexico in a preliminary round.

Cynics would attribute Australia's success to the large sums it invests in sports – AU$547 million in the four years before Athens. Perhaps it is no coincidence that of the forty-nine medals of all colours it won in 2004, thirty-five came from swimming, cycling, rowing and diving. All these disciplines benefited from hi-tech equipment developed at the Australian Institute of Sport. For example, the road cyclist Sara Carrigan trained in a 'sweat chamber' designed to mimic the humid conditions of the Greek summer. She then won gold wearing a gel-filled 'ice jacket' to keep her body from overheating. But the Australians are no slouches in non-Olympic sports either. They finished runners up in the 2003 Rugby World Cup, having won the contest four years earlier. They have also dominated Test cricket in recent years and won three consecutive Cricket World Cups in 1999, 2003 and 2007. Even without ploughing resources into Olympic success, the Australians enjoy a sunny climate conducive to long hours spent outdoors playing one sport or another. No doubt they would also thank their own optimism, patriotism and can-do attitude. The USA may be mistaken about its sporting prowess, but in these respects the real winners are every bit honorary Americans.

References

1. *Philosophical Investigations*, Oxford: Blackwell, 1953, §66

2. *Philosophy Of Science*, 1967, vol. 34, p. 148

3. *Wall Street Journal*, 5 September 2001

4. *Guardian*, 26 March 2002

5. Vialli, Gianluca and Marcotti, Gabriele, *The Italian Job*, London: Bantam, 2006, p. 61

6. BBC Sport, 2 March 1999

7. *Observer Sport Monthly*, May 2002

8. *New Yorker*, 19 May 1997

9. Entine, Jon, *Taboo: Why Black Athletes Dominate Sports and Why We're Afraid to Talk About It*, New York: Public Affairs, 2000

10. *Guardian Unlimited*, 3 September 2000

11. *New Statesman*, 8 September 2000

12. *Observer Sport Monthly*, 9 June 2002

13. *New Scientist*, 28 August 2004

14. Holden, Constance, 'Peering Under the Hood of Africa's Runners', *Science*, 30 July 2004, pp. 637–9

15. *Slate*, 30 November 2004

16. Associated Press, 9 August 2006

17 *Daily Telegraph*, 5 July 2006

18. BBC Online, 22 June 2005

19. *Sacramento Bee*, 7 June 2006

20. Gilovich, T., Vallone, R., and Tversky, A., 'The Hot Hand in Basketball: On the Misperception of Random Sequences', *Cognitive Psychology*, 1985, vol. 17, pp. 295–314

21. Clark, Russell D., 'An Examination of the "Hot Hand" in

Professional Golfers', *Perceptual and Motor Skills*, 2005, vol. 101/3, pp. 935–42

22. 'Spectator', *How To Win at Racing*, London: Raceform, 1987, p. 13

23. *London Review of Books*, 5 January 2006, vol. 28/1

24. *Star Tribune*, 2 February 1986

25. *Chicago Sun Times*, 14 April 2007

26. *Daily Mail*, 16 March 2007

27. *Independent on Sunday*, 6 May 2001

28. *Chicago Tribune*, 1 April 2007

29. *Private Eye*, no. 1181, 30 March–12 April 2007

30. *Electronic Telegraph*, 16 July 1996

31. Mehta, R. D., Bentley, K., Proudlove, M., and Varty, P., 'Factors Affecting Cricket Ball Swing', *Nature*, 1983, vol. 303, pp. 787–8

32. *Guardian*, 22 August 2006

33. www.cricinfo.com, 9 September 2006

34. *Business Day* (South Africa), 2 September 2006

35. Tatem, A. et al., *Nature*, vol. 431, p. 525

36. 'Gender Differences in Performance in Competitive Environments: Field Evidence from Professional Tennis Players', January 2007. Unpublished draft.

37. *International Herald Tribune*, 19 September 1996

38. BBC Sport, 30 July 2006

39. *Independent*, 7 October 2006

40. *International Herald Tribune*, 19 September 1996

41. *International Herald Tribune*, 11 May 2002

42. Pedoe, D. T., 'Sudden Cardiac Death in Sport – Spectre or Preventable Risk?', *British Journal of Sports Medicine*, 2000, vol. 34, pp. 137–40

43. Thompson, P. D., Funk, E. J., Carleton, R. A., and Sturner, W. Q., 'Incidence of Death During Jogging in Rhode Island from 1975

through 1980', *Journal of the American Medical Association*, 1982, vol. 247/18, pp. 2535–8

44. Siscovick, D., Weiss, N., Fletcher, R., and Lasky, T., 'The Incidence of Primary Cardiac Arrest During Vigorous Exercise', *The New England Journal of Medicine*, 1984, vol. 311/14, pp. 874–7

45. Noakes, T. D. 'Heart disease in marathon runners. A review.', *Medicine & Science in Sports & Exercise*, 1987, vol. 19, pp. 187–94.

46. Pedersen, B. K., and Toft, A. D., 'Effects of Exercise on Lymphocytes and Cytokines', *British Journal of Sports Medicine*, 2000, vol. 34, pp. 246–51

47. Schmitt, H., Rohs, C., Schneider, S., and Clarius, M., 'Is Competitive Running Associated with Osteoarthritis of the Hip or the Knee?', *Der Orthopäde*, October 2006, vol. 35/10, pp. 1087–92

48. Billat, V. et al., 'A Comparison of Time to Exhaustion at VO2 Max in Elite Cyclists, Kayak Paddlers, Swimmers and Runners', *Ergonomics*, February 1996, vol. 39/2, pp. 267–77

49. Neumann, G., 'Cycling', in Shephard, R.J., and Astrand, P. O., eds., *Endurance in Sport*, Oxford: Blackwell, 1992

50. *The Sun*, 31 July 2005

51. Heinicke, K. et al., 'A Three-Week Traditional Altitude Training Increases Hemoglobin Mass and Red Cell Volume in Elite Biathlon Athletes', *International Journal of Sports Medicine*, 2005, vol. 26, pp. 350–5

52. Walvin, J., *Football and the Decline of Britain*, Basingstoke: Macmillan, 1986

53. *Guardian*, 19 November 2005

54. Frosdick, S., and Marsh, P., *Football Hooliganism*, Willan Publishing, 2005

55. Quoted in *Football Hooliganism*

56. *Winning at any Cost: Doping in Sport*, National Commission on

Sports and Substance Abuse, Columbia University, 2000

57. Kayser, B., Mauron, A., and Miah, A., 'Viewpoint: Legalisation of Performance-Enhancing Drugs', *The Lancet*, 16 December 2005, vol. 366, Supplement 1:21

58. *Financial Times*, 11 February 2006

59. 10 February 2006

60. Savulescu, J., Foddy, B., and Clayton, M., 'Why We Should Allow Performance Enhancing Drugs in Sport', *British Journal of Sports Medicine*, December 2004, vol. 38, pp. 666–70

61. *Observer*, 8 August 2004

62. *Guardian*, 6 January 2003

63. *Independent*, 15 January 2006

64. *Independent*, 5 January 2006

65. BBC Online, 16 November 2000

66. *Independent*, 20 September 2003

67. *Daily Telegraph*, 27 August 2004

68. Reeser, J. C., 'Gender Identity and Sport: Is the Playing Field Level?', *British Journal of Sports Medicine*, 2005, vol. 39, pp. 695–9

69. *San Francisco Chronicle*, 14 June 2004

70. Vialli, Gianluca and Marcotti, Gabriele, *The Italian Job*, London: Bantam, 2006, p. 22

71. *Irish Times*, 15 November 2004

72. *Los Angeles Times*, 17 January 2007

73. *Pittsburgh Post-Gazette*, 15 February 1998

74. Ball, D .J., 'Assessing the Risks', *Sports Exercise and Injury*, 1998, vol. 4/1, pp. 3–9

75. Participation figures for mountaineering are based on the study *Participation in Sport*, Sport England, 2002

76. Ball, D. J., 'Assessing the Risks', *Sports Exercise and Injury*, 1998, vol. 4/1, pp. 3–9

77. *Daily Express*, 19 March 2007

78. *mX* (Australia), 7 July 2006

79. *New York Times*, 30 March 2007

80. Grouios, G. et al., 'Do Left-Handers Have an Innate Superiority in Sports?', *Perceptual and Motor Skills*, 2000, vol. 90, pp. 1273–82

81. *Neuropsychology*, November 2006, vol. 20/6

82. *New Scientist*, 8 December 2004

83. Source: www.anythingleft-handed.co.uk

84. Russell, Bill, *Second Wind*, New York: Random House, 1979

85. BBC Sport, 25 April 2006 and *Guardian*, 19 June 2006

86. *The Times*, 22 February 2007

87. *Guardian Unlimited*, 22 February 2007

88. Magee, Sean and Lewis, Guy, *To Win Just Once: The Life of a Journeyman Jump Jockey*, London: Headline, 1998

89. *Independent*, 14 November 2006 and the *Sunday Mirror*, 31 December 2006

90. *Guardian*, 14 November 2006

91. *Spectator*, 29 December 2001

92. Figures extracted from flatstats.co.uk

93. Figures extracted from the *Racing Post* database

94. *New Scientist*, no. 2500, 18 May 2005

95. Simonton, Dean Keith, *Greatness: Who Makes History and Why*, New York: Guilford Press, 1994

96. *The Times*, 1 June 2007

97. *Sun*, 16 February 2007

98. Source: www.thefa.com

99. 13 July 2006

100. Vialli, Gianluca and Marcotti, Gabriele, *The Italian Job*, London: Bantam, 2006, p. 71

101. Ibid., p. 74

102. *Scotsman*, 12 July 2006

103. *The Times*, 11 April 2003

104. Spurr, G. B., Dufour, D. L., and Reina, J. C., 'Increased Muscular Efficiency During Lactation in Colombian Women', *European Journal of Clinical Nutrition*, January 1998, vol. 52/1, pp. 17–21

105. *Scottish Daily Record*, 20 August 1999

106. BBC Sport, 11 April 2001

107. Source: www.premiersoccerstats.com

108. Linthorne, N. P., 'The Effect of Wind on 100-m Sprint Times', *Journal of Applied Biomechanics*, 1994, vol. 10/2, pp. 110–31

109. *The Herald*, 1 July 2006

110. *American Family Physician*, 1 June 2000

111. *New York Times*, 14 September 2006

112. Loucks, Anne B., and Nattiv, Aurelia, 'The Female Athlete Triad', *The Lancet*, 1 December 2005

113. Clarke, S., 'Home Advantage in Balanced Competitions: English Soccer 1991–6', Third Conference on Mathematics and Computers in Sports, 30 September–2 October 1996, Queensland, Australia, pp. 111–16

114. *Daily Mirror*, 17 November 2006

115. Zeller, R. A., and Jurkovac, T., 'Doming the Stadium: The Case for Baseball', *Sports Place International*, 1988, vol. 3, pp. 35–8

116. Ward, R.E. Jr, 'Rituals, First Impressions and the Opening Day Home Advantage', *Sociology of Sport Journal*, 1998, vol. 15, pp. 279–23

117. *New Scientist*, 16 March 2002

118. Nevill, A. M., Newell, S. M., and Gale, S., 'Factors Associated with Home Advantage in English and Scottish Soccer', *Journal of Sports Sciences*, 1996, vol. 14, pp. 181–6

119. *Sports Medicine*, vol. 28, 4 October 1999

120. *The Times*, 6 January 2004

121. *Evening Standard*, 26 January 2004

122. *Sun*, 27 December 2003

123. *Sports Illustrated*, 28 September 1999

124. *International Herald Tribune*, 10 January 1998

125. Weiland, Matt and Wilsey, Sean; eds., *The Thinking Fan's Guide to the World Cup*, London: Abacus, 2006

126. Metzl, Jordan D., MD; Small, Eric, MD; Levine, Steven R., MD; and Gershel, Jeffrey C., MD, 'Creatine Use Among Young Athletes', *Pediatrics*, vol. 108/2, August 2001, pp. 421–5

127. Keul, J., Deus, B., and Kindermann, W., 'Anabolic Steroids: Damages, Effect on Performance, and on Metabolism', *Medizinische Klinik*, March 19 1976, vol. 71/12, pp. 497–503

128. *New Scientist*, 12 August 2004

129. ibid

130. BBC News, 10 December 2005

131. *Pakistan Press International Information Services*, 7 December 2005

132. *Hindustan Times*, 1 December 2005

133. *Independent*, 28 October 1997

134. *Independent*, 25 February 2001

135. *Guardian*, 19 May 2007

136. *Cairns Post*, 29 March 2001

137. BBC Sport, 27 May 2002

138. *Daily Telegraph* (Australia), 16 June 2007

139. *Sunday Tribune*, 3 December 2006

140. *The Australian*, 14 June 2007

141. *New Zealand Herald*, 30 July 2007